listening
to the spirit

"What Is the Gospel Message to Our Church as We Relate to Gay and Lesbian Christians?"

listening
to the spirit

A HANDBOOK
FOR DISCERNMENT

William Paulsell, editor

CHALICE
PRESS

ST. LOUIS, MISSOURI

Bible quotations, unless otherwise noted, are from the *New Revised Standard Version Bible*, copyright 1989, Division of Christian Education of the National Council of Churches of Christ in the United States of America. Used by permission. All rights reserved.

Cover art: Chris Sharp
Cover design: Elizabeth Wright
Interior design: Hui-Chu Wang
Art direction: Michael Domínguez

This book is printed on acid-free, recycled paper.

Visit Chalice Press on the World Wide Web at
www.chalicepress.com

10 9 8 7 6 5 4 3 2 1   01 02 03 04 05 06

Library of Congress Cataloging–in–Publication Data

Listening to the Spirit : a handbook for discernment : "What is the Gospel message to our church as we relate to gay and lesbian Christians?" / William Paulsell, ed.
    p.   cm.
  Includes bibliographical references.
  ISBN 0-8272-2131-2 (alk. paper)
    1. Homosexuality—Religious aspects—Christian Church (Disciples of Christ) 2. Decision making—Religious aspects—Christian Church (Disciples of Christ) 3. Homosexuality—Religious aspects—Christian Church (Disciples of Christ)—Prayer-books and devotions—English. 4. Decision making—Religious aspects—Christian Church (Disciples of Christ)—Prayer-books and devotions—English. 5. Christian Church (Disciples of Christ)—Liturgy—Texts.   I. Paulsell, William O.
    BX7321.3 .L57 2001
  261.8'35766'088266—dc21

                                                    2001006020

Contents

Preface

As you begin working through this process of discernment, you may wonder why and how it was developed.

The genesis of this process was a request made by Park Avenue Christian Church in New York City to the General Assembly of the Christian Church (Disciples of Christ). The request was that the church address the question of the place of gay and lesbian persons in the life of the church.

In response, the Administrative Committee of the Disciples asked the General Minister and President, Richard Hamm, to appoint a steering committee that would be given two tasks: (1) to frame the issue for the church, and (2) to develop a process of discernment for the church to use in exploring the question raised by Park Avenue Christian Church.

Dr. Hamm appointed a committee of fourteen and employed a part-time staff person to work with the committee, which consisted of seven women and seven men. Among these people were two African Americans, two Hispanics, and one Asian. Seven of the members were at the time of their appointment pastors of local churches. Among the members were a regional staff person, a college chaplain, and a pastoral counselor. One held a doctoral degree in biblical studies. Four members were laity.

Three members of the group held conservative views on the question, believing that homosexuality is a sin. At the other end of the spectrum were three gay or lesbian members. In between were people who believed that they had much to learn about the whole question, as well as some who believed that the church should be more open to everyone. It was a well-balanced group, and virtually every position in the church was represented and heard.

The committee met periodically for two and a half years, with members working between meetings on various aspects of the discernment process. The development of the process evolved as the group worshiped, engaged in Bible study, and shared personal stories.

Although there were major differences of opinion on the committee, the common bond was a love for the church and a deep commitment to the Christian gospel. Every meeting ended with a service of the Lord's supper. In coming to the table together, the committee was saying that everyone's faith and integrity were understood and respected. As the group continued to meet, a sense of love and appreciation emerged that transcended differences of opinion on the place of gay and lesbian persons in the life of the church. That was one of the wonderful gifts of the Holy Spirit to the committee.

The committee discussed many different aspects of the issues, but finally came to the conclusion that the fundamental question is, "What is the gospel message to our church as we relate to gay and lesbian Christians?" For the committee, this question outweighed all other issues.

Although this process was developed by members of the Christian Church (Disciples of Christ), it should be useful in virtually any denominational tradition. The committee hopes that this will be a valuable experience for you and that you will sense the leading of the Holy Spirit.

Gregory Alexander	Lexington, Kentucky
Mark Johnston	Boston, Massachusetts
Dana Bainbridge	Omaha, Nebraska
JoAnne Kagiwada	Oakland, California
Peter Browning	Springfield, Missouri
Diane Paulsell	Princeton, New Jersey
Jo Ann Bynum	Los Angeles, California
Maria Perez	Bronx, New York
David Cortes	Deltona, Florida
Douglas Skinner	Dallas, Texas
Ronald Greene	Spokane, Washington
Mary Smith	West Glacier, Montana
Alvin Jackson	Washington, D.C.
Judith Hoch Wray	New York City, New York
William Paulsell	Lexington, Kentucky

Introduction

Gay and lesbian people are present in our society and in our churches. Although many keep their sexual orientation secret for fear of discrimination, job loss, alienation from family, or violence, many are much more open now about their lives.

The fact that there are gay and lesbian people in the church has raised many questions. Are there any reasons why gay and lesbian Christians should not be treated as other Christians? Should the church ordain gay and lesbian persons as ministers? Should gay and lesbian persons hold offices in local churches? What does the Bible have to teach us on these questions?

Such questions are difficult for the church, and the controversy surrounding them is painful for many. It is painful for those who believe that the issue is resolved and who fear that more discussion may compromise their faith or their relationship with their church. It is painful for churches and denominations that are divided. It is painful for families with lesbian and gay members and for gay and lesbian people who face discrimination and condemnation. The church is attempting to respond by receiving the light of scripture and by listening to the Holy Spirit.

What should the people of God do in situations of such conflict and pain? How should decisions be made in the church?

One way that many churches make decisions when facing a difficult question is to debate and vote. There are winners and losers. The winners think the matter has been resolved. The losers refuse to let go of it. Bad feelings are generated, and unity within and between congregations is fractured. A better way to respond to this pain and confusion is to make use of a process of discernment. Such a process assumes that the Holy Spirit is at work in the church. Discernment is a matter of listening to the Spirit for guidance in our church life.

This process of discernment is designed to help us listen to God as we consider the question, What is the gospel message to our church as we relate to gay and lesbian Christians?

Every Christian is called to live the gospel faithfully and fully. That is the focus of this process, which could have taken many different paths. A wealth of information is available about related scientific, sociological, and cultural issues. This information will inevitably be part of what each participant brings to this process. In the process of discernment, however, the steering committee chose to focus on how to live the gospel.

What Is Discernment?

*Do not be conformed to this world, but be transformed
by the renewing of your minds, so that you may discern
what is the will of God—what is good and acceptable
and perfect. Romans 12:2*

Rather than trying to solve problems by debate and vote, discernment takes a different approach, one of listening to the Holy Spirit. In this process you will study some biblical passages in which you will read of the early church's efforts to discern how the Spirit was leading the church to face difficult issues.

Through worship, Bible study, sharing personal stories, and gathering around the Lord's table, you can begin to hear what the Spirit is saying. When you discern, you do not argue or debate, but listen respectfully to each other in the hope that through these experiences you will hear the Spirit and discern the will of God.

In his book *Scripture and Discernment,* Luke Timothy Johnson writes, "The entire point of hearing the stories of individuals and groups as they are gathered by shared experiences is to discover how God is acting in the world."[1]

This process is going to take some time. How much time depends on the experience of the group engaging in the discernment process. You may plan to meet once a week until the process is completed. You may have a weekend retreat to work through some or all of the sessions. Whatever schedule is used, you must be willing to take the time needed for the process to work.

---

[1]Luke Timothy Johnson, *Scripture and Discernment* (Nashville: Abingdon Press, 1996), 112.

The process may be engaged by the leaders of a congregation, by the church board, or by any small group. It may be used by a regional committee on the ministry or a regional board, by a group in one of our general units, or by a campus student group. There are many possibilities. You have to decide what works best for your congregation or organization. It is *essential* that in whatever group uses the process, there is participation by gay and lesbian persons. The process will not have integrity if lesbian and gay voices are not heard.

This process assumes no specific outcome. That will be determined by the Holy Spirit. In the gospel of John, Jesus says, "The wind blows where it chooses, and you hear the sound of it, but you do not know where it comes from or where it goes. So it is with everyone who is born of the Spirit" (3:8). The process does assume that the Holy Spirit is at work in your midst, but no one can predict what the Spirit will do.

The basic intention of the process is to help you develop a sensitivity to the Spirit. The hope is that as you struggle with how to relate to gay and lesbian Christians, you will receive guidance from the Spirit. This requires careful and thoughtful listening to one another, to the Bible, and to that still, small voice that you encounter in worship and communion.

Ruth Fletcher wrote a book about discernment for the office of the Disciples' General Minister and President called *Take, Break, Receive: The Practice of Discernment in the Christian Church (Disciples of Christ).*[2] Her opening chapter is on "Discernment in the Christian Tradition." The rest of this chapter of the manual consists of her understanding of discernment.

Discernment has to do with sifting through the information we've been given in order to make sense of it. For centuries, Christians have used the word *discernment* to describe the prayerful process of seeking God's leading in their individual lives and in the life of the church. That seeking, that longing to know God's heart, points to the reality of our human condition: We can enter into the loving, creative mystery in which life is created, bathed, and nurtured;

---

[2]Ruth Fletcher, *Take, Break, Receive: The Practice of Discernment in the Christian Church (Disciples of Christ).* Available from the Division of Homeland Ministries, P. O. Box 1986, Indianapolis, Indiana 46206-1986.

we can orient ourselves toward a hope that transcends our own vision.

Through the ages, when followers of Jesus Christ have found themselves at crossroads, they have turned to scripture study, prayer, and theological reflection in order to seek God's guidance. Those disciplines have helped the faithful to see more clearly where and how God is at work in the world and to discover how they can participate more fully in that work, offering healing, love, and peace.

Today the church is rediscovering the value of discernment as a practice that can offer practical help in confusing times. It is reclaiming the discipline as a means of making personal choices and inspiring deeper faithfulness. Discernment can generate vitality and courage as we imagine, reflect, and make decisions together about the future shape and direction of our common life and mission. As we work through the steps of a process, we can learn to distinguish the voice of the Holy One from all the other voices that seek to influence us, so we can make sound decisions and act, as much as possible, in accordance with God's intentions. Discernment is the way we live out the prayer we pray each Sunday, "Thy will be done."

Discernment is not a new fad; it is an ancient practice that has it roots in the early church. Acts 15 gives us a glimpse into one of the first occasions the church enters into a discernment process, in which Paul and Barnabas travel to Jerusalem in order to pose a question to the apostles and elders of the church. [Acts 15 will be studied in stage 6.] As the church grew over time, men and women who chose to live in religious communities searched for ways to be faithful to the leading of the Spirit.

After the Reformation, other models of communal discernment evolved among Protestants. Leaders such as Luther, Calvin, and Zwingli focused on scripture as the primary means by which God's will was revealed. Later, the Society of Friends (Quakers) added their own forms to the practice of discernment as they "waited upon the Spirit." They learned to come to consensus. They created the "clearness committee" (gathering a group of trusted people together to listen and reflect with an individual who is trying to make a choice). When not everyone agreed about which direction the Spirit was leading, they discovered value in registering nonconcurrence.

Other Protestant groups continued making time to come together as Christians to follow the leading of the Spirit. In 1792, founders of the Methodist movement formed the Covenant Group called a "Holy Club," whose members encouraged each other in practicing the disciplines of prayer, Bible study, fasting, communion, and service. They believed that the Spirit works within each individual from the time of baptism, helping that person to grow in faith and discipleship.

Early founders of the movement that eventually became the Christian Church (Disciples of Christ) emphasized the importance of the biblical story in the discernment process. They believed the Holy Spirit to be an active agent that "subdues chaos, brings order, and vitalizes humanity," shaping the character of Christians and helping them to come to know God more fully through the scriptures. According to Alexander Campbell, those who wished to discern God's will should open the Bible with that aim as their ardent desire and sole intent. With that focus in mind, he believed that those who would go seeking for guidance would not be disappointed.

The language of the Spirit is unfamiliar. Often, we see God's hand in our lives only in retrospect, looking backward from a safe place. While we're in the middle of it, the process of discernment can feel chaotic, at times nebulous. That means that there will be people in every congregation who will be uncomfortable with the practice of discernment. Those who are used to business meetings, which rely mostly on logic and persuasive debate, may find it especially uncomfortable to work in a mode that requires the group to attend to an insight here, a feeling there, a sense of being on the verge of something everywhere.

Yet that is the countercultural character of the discernment process. It goes against the norms of individualism, competition, compartmentalization, and specialization that have become such familiar parts of our secularized culture.

Instead, it seeks to build community and consensus. It challenges the concept of church as one of a number of nice community activities, calling instead for Christians to take seriously those practices of Bible study, prayer, and reflective listening, which can lead to radical transformation and singular commitment to doing God's will.

Preparation for Discernment

Choosing Leaders

A leader should be chosen who is respected in the congregation or group and who does not have a personal agenda to impose on others. A pastor will have to make a decision regarding his or her participation. It is important that the pastor maintain a pastoral role in a situation in which there may be tension and disagreement.

The leader should read this entire manual and become familiar with it and the video material before taking the leadership of a group.

Personal Preparation

The process requires a serious time commitment. A matter of such difficulty and importance to the church should not be dealt with superficially. We invite you to take this journey, to follow the suggestions, to listen to the Spirit. Please take your time with the process. Do not become impatient and rush to complete it. It takes time to develop a sensitivity to the Holy Spirit and to one another.

There is no preconceived outcome to this process. The whole purpose is to listen to the Holy Spirit. This requires that people come with openness and a willingness to listen to others.

Forming a Group

The ideal group should have no fewer than six people and no more than twelve. Once the process has begun, no new people should be added to the group. If others want to participate, a new group should be formed. A larger group may share opening and closing worship and then divide into smaller groups for Bible study and discussion. The same persons should gather in each small group at each meeting.

To stay true to the process, it is essential that gay and lesbian people be members of the group from the beginning. Their voices must be heard for the process to have integrity. See the resources list at the end of this manual for help in finding gay and lesbian Christians.

Creating a Safe Space

As you come together, your space needs to be safe for everyone. Only in this way can everyone share thoughts and feelings about the question for discernment. In order to create a safe space, this discernment process includes four rules for safe space, which are closely related to the rules for discernment:

1. Honor each person as a person of faith.

2. Gather to listen.

3. Protect what is shared.

4. Find your unity in Christ.

When you honor one another as people of faith, you recognize that God can speak to you even through those with whom you disagree, and you listen for the word that God has for your group in what others have to say.

Furthermore, as you gather to listen, you acknowledge that a discernment process is not about convincing others that you are right, but is listening for the message God has for your group. When you contribute your thoughts, opinions, and feelings, do this to share yourself, not to convince others. When making statements, be clear that you are sharing a thought or an opinion rather than trying to argue for your viewpoint. If you find yourself speaking often, try to spend more time listening. If others are quiet, encourage them to speak. Allow others to complete their sharing without interrupting or asking questions.

As you share yourself, protect what is shared. Information, thoughts, and feelings shared in the group must remain confidential within the group. Also, avoid sharing information about others who are not in the group. If a story about someone else will contribute to the discussion, only share that story if that person can be kept safe by maintaining her or his confidentiality. Do not reveal that someone you know is lesbian or gay if that person would not want that information known or if you are unsure about whether the person would want the information known.

In all your sharing, remember that it is Christ who makes Christians one. People continue to be members of the one church even when there is disagreement about doctrine or other issues.

When the focus is on unity in Christ, you can create a safe space for one another so that everyone can listen for the word God has for you and your group.

In the opening worship for each session, a Litany of the One Spirit, which commits the group to the rules for creating safe space, is included.

How to Use This Process

You have been provided with this manual and a videotape to guide you through this process. Every participant should have a copy of the manual and should read it in preparation for each stage. By following these instructions carefully, you will be able to explore at a much deeper level than you have before the question of how to relate to lesbian and gay Christians.

Four basic activities make up each session: worship, personal sharing, Bible study, and the Lord's supper. We have provided simple liturgies to be used for worship and the Lord's supper. If a stage has to be divided into several sessions, worship and the Lord's supper should be part of each session. Every time the group meets, worship and communion should be part of the shared experience. The worship for each stage can be repeated as often as necessary.

There are seven stages in this process, each building on the previous one. You may discover that some stages require several sessions. In some of the stages, you will find suggestions for dividing the material. How to divide the material depends on what the group experiences at each session. There may be times when you will want to spend additional time on a particular stage. Be flexible. It is important that the process not be rushed, for it takes time to develop a sensitivity to the Holy Spirit.

The meeting room should be set up with a communion table or worship center that should always be present when the group meets. For opening worship, suggestions are made for items to be placed on the table at each stage. Leave the items from previous stages on the table so that important symbols will accumulate as you proceed through the process. Turning your attention to God in worship will keep the whole process in a spiritual context rather than a debate context, and will help participants become better listeners.

Personal sharing is one of the most important parts of this process. The telling and hearing of personal stories may be one of the ways through which the Holy Spirit speaks to you. There may be times when an additional session will need to be added in order to allow everyone time to tell his or her story.

Each stage has Bible passages to be studied, along with some interpretative helps and questions for discussion. Biblical material should always be read by the participants before each session. Stage 1 offers some basic principles of biblical interpretation that will help you discover the meanings of the passages studied. It is important to the discernment process to review these from time to time so that they will be used and not be forgotten.

In every session the group will renew a covenant that includes fundamental principles for discernment. It is very important that this covenant be renewed each time so that discernment rather than debate will take place.

Each time you meet, your time together should conclude with a brief service of the Lord's supper. A simple liturgy has been provided, containing the essentials. You may develop it, expand it, or use it as it is. Because many differences of opinion will be expressed during the session, it is important that you come to the table together to reaffirm that every person in the group is a member of the body of Christ and an object of the love of God.

At each session people should be assigned to lead worship and the communion service at the next session. Note that the discussion of question 4 in stage 5 requires some art supplies.

As you work through the process and engage in worship, personal sharing, Bible study, and communion, keep in mind that this process is about answering the question, What is the gospel message to our church as we relate to gay and lesbian Christians? The conversation may stray to other issues and questions, and it will be necessary to refocus the conversation on this question. While many related questions and issues could be discussed, the purpose of this process is to discern how to relate to people, to Christians, who are lesbian or gay.

No matter what your opinion on this basic question may be, you will encounter ideas in this manual and in the personal sharing with which you will disagree. Acknowledge that honestly, but do not leave the process. Keep the covenant to stay with the process to the end. You are not asked to agree with everyone, but you are asked to listen to others and to the Holy Spirit.

May God bless you as you work with this process, and may the Holy Spirit's presence and leading become clearer to you.

Introduction to the Process of Discernment

This stage contains two major Bible studies. If you are meeting in an extended retreat setting, you should have no problem covering all the material. However, if you are meeting in a series of evening sessions, you will want to divide this stage into at least two sessions, using part 1 in the first and part 2 in the second. Remember that the opening worship and closing communion service should be used each time you meet.

OPENING WORSHIP

LITANY OF THE ONE SPIRIT

We call upon the Spirit of God to gather us together.
We honor the Spirit of God, dwelling in each of us.
We come to listen to one another.
And we come to listen for the Spirit who dwells within us all.
We honor this space as the place where God calls us together.
We cherish and protect what is shared in this space.
We find our unity in the One God, not in doctrine or
argument.
We honor our unity in Christ.
To the One whom we honor and praise,
the One God who is Love. Amen.

INVOCATION [in unison]

O God, we have come together to walk with you, as did the disciples of old, along our own Emmaus

Road. We pray that the fears and uncertainties that cloud our minds may be dispelled by your words. Bless our shared journey in the simple and sacred act of the breaking of bread. Amen.

LIGHTING OF A CANDLE

God's Word is a lamp to our feet
and a light to our path.
We light this candle to remind us that we do not make this journey alone.
[Light candle here.]
May God light our way. Amen.

INTRODUCTIONS

Ask each person to introduce herself or himself and to share a self-descriptive word or phrase.

STATEMENT OF COVENANT

God, as facilitator of this discussion, invites us to enter into a covenant with God and with one another.
In response to God's invitation:
I will honor and respect every participant as a person of faith.
I will claim a shared belief that the Holy Spirit is present and at work in this community.
I will examine the whole of scripture, not just isolated verses.
I will earnestly seek to hear and understand perspectives different from my own.
I will seek to retain a unity of Spirit even when I disagree.
As God's church, this will be a safe and confidential place where people can discuss sensitive issues freely without feeling that they will be attacked or rejected. Amen.

PART 1: Discernment in the Bible

Bible Study

We turn to Acts 10 to discover how the early church discerned the will of God. As you listen to the text being read, note the discernment process taking place and the factors that led to the making of a decision. *(Invite one or more persons in your group to read the following text aloud:)*

Acts 10:1–48

¹In Caesarea there was a man named Cornelius, a centurion of the Italian Cohort, as it was called. ²He was a devout man who feared God with all his household; he gave alms generously to the people and prayed constantly to God. ³One afternoon at about three o"clock he had a vision in which he clearly saw an angel of God coming in and saying to him, "Cornelius."

⁴He stared at him in terror and said, "What is it, Lord?" He answered, "Your prayers and your alms have ascended as a memorial before God. ⁵Now send men to Joppa for a certain Simon who is called Peter; ⁶he is lodging with Simon, a tanner, whose house is by the seaside."

⁷When the angel who spoke to him had left, he called two of his slaves and a devout soldier from the ranks of those who served him, ⁸and after telling them everything, he sent them to Joppa.

⁹About noon the next day, as they were on their journey and approaching the city, Peter went up on the roof to pray. ¹⁰He became hungry and wanted something to eat; and while it was being prepared, he fell into a trance. ¹¹He saw the heaven opened and something like a large sheet coming down, being lowered to the ground by its four corners. ¹²In it were all kinds of four-footed creatures and reptiles and birds of the air. ¹³Then he heard a voice saying, "Get up, Peter; kill and eat." ¹⁴But Peter said, "By no means, Lord; for I have never eaten anything that is profane or unclean." ¹⁵The voice said to him again, a second time, "What God has made clean, you must not call profane." ¹⁶This happened three times, and the thing was suddenly taken up to heaven.

¹⁷Now while Peter was greatly puzzled about what to make of the vision that he had seen, suddenly the men sent by Cornelius appeared. They were asking for Simon's house and were standing by the gate. ¹⁸They called out to ask whether Simon, who was called Peter, was staying there. ¹⁹While Peter was still thinking about the vision, the Spirit said to him, "Look, three men are searching for you. ²⁰Now get up, go down, and go with them without hesitation; for I have sent them."

21So Peter went down to the men and said, "I am the one you are looking for; what is the reason for your coming?"

22They answered, "Cornelius, a centurion, an upright and God-fearing man, who is well spoken of by the whole Jewish nation, was directed by a holy angel to send for you to come to his house and to hear what you have to say."

23So Peter invited them in and gave them lodging.

The next day he got up and went with them, and some of the believers from Joppa accompanied him.

24The following day they came to Caesarea. Cornelius was expecting them and had called together his relatives and close friends. 25On Peter's arrival Cornelius met him, and falling at his feet, worshiped him. 26But Peter made him get up, saying, "Stand up; I am only a mortal."

27And as he talked with him, he went in and found that many had assembled; 28and he said to them, "You yourselves know that it is unlawful for a Jew to associate with or to visit a Gentile; but God has shown me that I should not call anyone profane or unclean. 29So when I was sent for, I came without objection. Now may I ask why you sent for me?"

30Cornelius replied, "Four days ago at this very hour, at three o'clock, I was praying in my house when suddenly a man in dazzling clothes stood before me. 31He said, 'Cornelius, your prayer has been heard and your alms have been remembered before God. 32Send therefore to Joppa and ask for Simon, who is called Peter; he is staying in the home of Simon, a tanner, by the sea.' 33Therefore I sent for you immediately, and you have been kind enough to come. So now all of us are here in the presence of God to listen to all that the Lord has commanded you to say."

34Then Peter began to speak to them: "I truly understand that God shows no partiality, 35but in every nation anyone who fears God and does what is right is acceptable to God. 36You know the message God sent to the people of Israel, preaching peace by Jesus Christ–he is Lord of all. 37That message spread throughout Judea, beginning in Galilee after the baptism that John announced: 38how God anointed Jesus of Nazareth with the Holy Spirit and with power; how he went about doing good and healing all who were oppressed by the devil, for God was with him. [39]We are witnesses to all that he did both in Judea and in Jerusalem. They put him to death by hanging him on a tree; [40]but God raised him on the third day and allowed him to appear, [41]not to all the people but to us who were chosen by God as witnesses, and who ate and drank with him after he rose from the dead. [42]He commanded us to preach to the people and to testify that he is the one ordained by God as judge of the living and the dead. [43]All the prophets testify about him that everyone who believes in him receives forgiveness of sins through his name."

[44]While Peter was still speaking, the Holy Spirit fell upon all who heard the word. [45]The circumcised believers who had come with Peter were astounded that the gift of the Holy Spirit had been poured out even on the Gentiles, [46]for they heard them speaking in tongues and extolling God. Then Peter said, [47]"Can anyone withhold the water for baptizing these people who have received the Holy Spirit just as we have?" [48]So he ordered them to be baptized in the name of Jesus Christ. Then they invited him to stay for several days.

For discussion

(1) Many different people are involved in this text, which speaks of a change in how God's people understood God's will. As a group, list the different persons and groups of people named in the text.

(2) Divide into three groups. One group is to discuss the following questions from the perspective of Cornelius; one group from the perspective of Simon Peter; and the other group from the perspective of the believers from Joppa. Remember that the focus of this Bible study is on *the process* of discernment.

(a) What was the process of insight for Cornelius? (or Peter? or believers from Joppa?)

(b) What were the obstacles to insight?

(c) In what ways is this or is this not about discernment?

(d) What conclusions/questions from your group discussion of this text are pertinent to our discernment about the gospel message to our church as we relate to lesbian and gay Christians?

(3) Come back together. Invite someone from each group to share insights from the small group discussions.

PART 2: Introduction to Bible Study

Invite one or more group members to read aloud the Basic Principles of Biblical Interpretation presented here. Watch the video discussion of these principles.

Basic Principles of Biblical Interpretation

The Word

The Word of God is Jesus the Christ. Scripture is effectively Word when, in the light of the gospel, we hear God's covenant of love with all people in both the Old and New Testaments. The life, ministry, teaching, death, resurrection, and continuing presence of Jesus the Christ is the filter through which we finally discern the significance of the varied witnesses of scripture.

Canon

The canon of scripture (all the books of the Bible) provides us with a way of keeping all our diverse communities of faith within hearing distance of the others. Disciples of Christ understand the importance of weighing the whole counsel of God when deciding matters of faith and practice, rather than depending on isolated proof-texts.

The witness of the whole Bible serves to modify and correct the witness of individual parts. For example, certain biblical texts deny the possibility of resurrection (See Ps. 115:17; Eccl. 9:5). However, the general witness of the scriptures and the testimony concerning Jesus the Christ affirm, proclaim, and expect the resurrection.

Community

No one is impartial in her or his reading and interpretation of scripture. Life experience and received teaching inform the way we see, hear, and understand God's word. As Christians, we study scripture in community, not so that those in authority may define how others understand the texts, but so that the perspectives and insights of the community may inform and enlighten the whole body together. The Holy Spirit comes upon the whole community. When we do biblical interpretation in community, with the whole people of God, we can receive the gift of multifaceted perspectives. Humility is the order of the day, lest we find ourselves, like Job, needing to confess that "I have uttered what I did not understand, things too wonderful for me, which I did not know" (Job 42:3b).

Genre

The interpretation of a text of scripture will be shaped by its literary form. Parables require a different approach than prayers. A knowledge of characteristics and function of apocalyptic literature is indispensable for a responsible reading of Daniel or Revelation. The gospels are not to be read as biographies. The New Testament presents faith accounts, not historical reports, of the life of Jesus the Christ and of the early church. Thus, the synoptic gospels (Matthew, Mark, Luke) frequently present different accounts of the same event, nuanced to emphasize the faith teaching needed by the different communities to which each gospel account was written.

Contexts

The biblical texts were written in particular sociohistorical contexts. To discern God's wisdom for a different sociohistorical context, the dynamics and implications of the original context must be considered. For example, we no longer require non-Jews to become circumcised in order to become Christians. We no longer quote the Bible to justify slavery. Most Christians no longer feel a need to obey the purity laws that forbid the eating of pork or shellfish.

The meaning of any given text is conditioned by its immediate scriptural context. For example, someone can accurately say that the Bible says, "There is no God." However, the context corrects that reading: "Fools say in their hearts, 'There is no God'" (Ps 14:1; 53:1).

Spirit

In order to hear God's word responsibly, as we approach scripture we must acknowledge our dependence on and expectation of the Holy Spirit to illuminate the words and transform those of us who listen for God's truths.

Alexander Campbell's Seven Rules of Biblical Interpretation

Alexander Campbell believed in a Bible that was authoritative for Christian faith and practice, but that at the same time had to be carefully interpreted. He believed that in order for the Bible to exercise its authority, its message should be properly understood in its original context and then carefully applied to the reader's. To help readers of the Bible do this important work of careful interpretation, Campbell offered seven rules for the interpretation of scripture in *The Christian System* (1835). These rules of interpretation placed our spiritual tradition in the stream of biblical criticism in which we remain to this day.

Campbell's first rule of interpretation reflects his historical consciousness. This rule concerns the importance of understanding the historical circumstances of the composition of the biblical text.

> **RULE 1:** On opening any book in the sacred Scriptures, consider first the historical circumstances of the book. These are the order, the title, the author, the date, the place, and the occasion of it.

In other words, Campbell insists that responsible interpretation of any text requires understanding where the biblical book is placed within the Bible as a whole, an awareness of the book's title, who actually wrote the book, when it was written, where it was written and to whom, as well as the reason the writer chose to address the specific topics in the book.

Campbell's second rule of interpretation reflects his understanding of the fact that the story of salvation unfolds in successive stages, or dispensations, with one covenant superseding another.

> **RULE 2:** In examining the contents of any book, as respects precepts, promises, exhortations, etc., observe who it is that speaks, and under what dispensation he officiates.

Campbell believes that biblical texts have various levels of authority for Christians. He is convinced, for example, that New Testament texts carry more weight for Christians, because he believes the that the new covenant in Christ supersedes the covenants found in the Old Testament and that the words of some biblical writers are more prescriptive for Christians than the words of other biblical writers. Although not all Christians adopt this "supercessionary" view, the idea that various texts should be given different authoritative weights remains a key principle.

Campbell's third and fourth rules of interpretation ask readers to approach the scriptures as they would any book, with all the principles of language and grammar in effect.

> **RULE 3:** To understand the meaning of what is commanded, promised, taught, etc., the same philological principles,

deduced from the nature of language; or the same laws of interpretation which are applied to the language of other books, are to be applied to the language of the Bible.

RULE 4: Common usage, which can only be ascertained by testimony, must always decide the meaning of any word which has but one signification; but when words have, according to testimony (i.e., the dictionary,) more meanings than one, whether literal or figurative, the scope, the context, or parallel passages must decide the meaning; for if common usage, the design of the writer, the context, and parallel passages fail, there can be no certainty in the interpretation of language.

Campbell insists that in order to understand a text properly, the interpreter must pay attention to the dynamics of language: grammar, syntax, and the history and meaning of the words themselves. Thus, responsible Bible study will include careful word studies, examination of the context and of parallel passages, and an awareness that some texts are to be interpreted literally while others are to be understood figuratively. Campbell recognizes that in some instances we do not have enough information to determine the true meaning of a text.

In rules 5 and 6, Campbell shows his impatience with a mystical or allegorical reading of the biblical text.

RULE 5: In all tropical language, ascertain the point of resemblance, and judge the nature of the trope, and its kind, from the point of resemblance.

RULE 6: In the interpretation of symbols, types, allegories, and parables, this rule is supreme: Ascertain the point to be illustrated; for comparison is never to be extended beyond that point—to all the attributes, qualities, or circumstances of the symbol, type, allegory, or parable.

A *trope* (hence, "tropical language") is a word or expression used figuratively, a word or expression used in a different sense from what it ordinarily possesses, a figure of speech. Campbell urges the interpreter to refrain from flights of fanciful comparison that would extend the meaning far beyond the basic illustration implied in the text.

Campbell's seventh rule of interpretation calls for a stance of humility and a spirit of expectancy in the interpretive process.

RULE 7: For the salutary and sanctifying intelligence of the Oracles of God, the following rule is indispensable: We must come within the understanding distance. There is a distance which is properly called the speaking distance, or the hearing distance; beyond which the voice reaches not, and the ear hears not. To hear another, we must come within that circle which the voice audibly fills.

Now we may with propriety say, that as respects God, there is an understanding distance. All beyond that distance cannot understand God; all within it can easily understand him in all matters of piety and morality. God is the center of that circle, and humility is its circumference.

Campbell believed that in order to receive the full benefits available from faithful Bible study, the interpreter must approach the text with expectancy, open to the possibility that God will indeed speak and that the interpreter will indeed hear guidance from God's Spirit. In all biblical study, humility is the order of the day. God, not our own wisdom, is the center of all faithful interpretation.

Campbell also believed that by using these rules of interpretation, the words and ideas of the Bible could be widely understood. Without these rules of interpretation, Campbell argued, the meaning of the scriptures would depend on the interpretations of "an inspired class...to unfold and reveal its true sense." But with these rules in their heads and hearts, every Christian believer is empowered to be an interpreter of scripture, which is exactly what Campbell wants—the church as a community of interpreters.

The following Bible study exercise will help everyone involved in the discernment process understand the significance of these basic principles and of Campbell's rules. The texts you are being asked to work with in this exercise have been deliberately chosen because (1) they are completely unrelated to the issue under consideration by this discernment process, and (2) they present some rather interesting interpretive challenges. The goal is not to find the "correct" interpretation of the following texts, but rather (1) to experience the way that using these principles and rules affects the interpretive process, (2) to identify the kinds of questions that these principles and rules will ordinarily prompt in a faithful interpreter, and (3) to name some of the kinds of resources that are available to the faithful interpreter. The value of this exercise in interpretation using the basic principles and Campbell's rules is the way that it can inform the group's Bible studies during each stage of the discernment process, especially in stage 4, when you will take a good look at the texts that have been understood as addressing homosexuality.

Invite someone to read the following texts aloud:

Ecclesiastes 9:1–10

[1]All this I laid to heart, examining it all, how the righteous and the wise and their deeds are in the hand of God; whether it is love or hate one does not know. Everything that confronts them [2]is vanity, since the same fate comes to all, to the righteous and the wicked, to the good and the evil, to the clean and the unclean, to those who sacrifice and those who do not sacrifice. As are the good, so are the sinners; those who swear are like those who shun an oath. [3]This is an evil in all that happens under the sun, that the same fate comes to everyone. Moreover, the hearts of all are full of evil; madness is in their hearts while they live, and after that they go to the dead. [4]But whoever is joined with all the living has hope, for a living dog is better than a dead lion. [5]The living know that they will die, but the dead know nothing; they have no more reward, and even the memory of them is lost. [6]Their love and their hate and their envy have already perished; never again will they have any share in all that happens under the sun.

[7]Go, eat your bread with enjoyment, and drink your wine with a merry heart; for God has long ago approved what you do. [8]Let your garments always be white; do not let oil be lacking on your head. [9]Enjoy life with the wife whom you love, all the days of your vain life that are given you under the sun because that is your portion in life and in your toil at which you toil under the sun. [10]Whatever your hand finds to do, do with your might; for there is no work or thought or knowledge or wisdom in Sheol, to which you are going.

1 Corinthians 7:21–24

Were you a slave when called? Do not be concerned about it. Even if you can gain your freedom, make use of your present condition now more than ever. For whoever was called in the Lord as a slave is a freed person belonging to the Lord, just as whoever was free when called is a slave of Christ. You were bought with a price; do not become slaves of human masters. In whatever condition you were called, brothers and sisters, there remain with God.

For discussion

Examine the two texts, one at a time, using the following questions:

In light of our interpretative heritage reflected in the basic principles of biblical interpretation and Alexander Campbell's seven rules of biblical interpretation, what questions should we ask in order to come to a faithful interpretation of this text? Which principles of biblical interpretation seem to be pertinent to the understanding of each text? Identify how these principles will affect the interpretive process of these texts.

After the group has worked with each of these texts, discuss the following questions:

What new insights occur to you as you work with these principles of interpretation?

How will an awareness of the kinds of questions needed for faithful Bible study affect your own biblical interpretative process?

CLOSING WORSHIP

Hymn

Communion

Words of Institution: 1 Corinthians 11:23–26
Prayer for the loaf and the cup
Partaking of the loaf and the cup

Closing Prayer

O God, we have begun a new faith journey together. Bless each step we take, we pray. Send us forth in your peace, assured that you will journey with us. Amen.

Benediction

As you depart, say to one another, "God be with you till we meet again."

Spiritual Preparation for Discernment

OPENING WORSHIP

LITANY OF THE ONE SPIRIT

> We call upon the Spirit of God to gather us together.
> **We honor the Spirit of God, dwelling in each of us.**
> We come to listen to one another.
> **And we come to listen for the Spirit who dwells within us all.**
> We honor this space as the place where God calls us together.
> **We cherish and protect what is shared in this space.**
> We find our unity in the One God, not in doctrine or argument.
> **We honor our unity in Christ.**
> **To the One whom we honor and praise,**
> **the One God who is Love. Amen.**

INVOCATION (in unison)

> **O God, as we continue our journey together, open us to the leading of your Spirit. Place us within a safe listening distance of our traveling companions so that together we may discern your will. Bless our shared journey in the simple and sacred act of the breaking of bread. Amen.**

LIGHTING OF A CANDLE

> God's Word is a lamp to our feet
> **and a light to our path.**

We light this candle to remind us that we do not make this journey alone.

[Light candle here.]

May God light our way. Amen.

STATEMENT OF COVENANT

God, as facilitator of this discussion, invites us to enter into a covenant with God and with one another.

In response to God's invitation:

I will honor and respect every participant as a person of faith.

I will claim a shared belief that the Holy Spirit is present and at work in this community.

I will examine the whole of scripture, not just isolated verses.

I will earnestly seek to hear and understand perspectives different from my own.

I will seek to retain a unity of Spirit even when I disagree.

As God's church, this will be a safe and confidential place where people can discuss sensitive issues freely without feeling that they will be attacked or rejected. Amen.

PLACING OF THE CROSS

Place a cross on the worship center table. Ask one person to read the following.

In this stage we discuss our concerns, our fears, and our prejudices. The cross is a symbol of the Christian journey of faith. At the cross we are confronted with sin, with violence, and with forgiveness and hope. At the cross we are empowered to let go of whatever binds our spirits and inhibits the deepening of our faith.

Bible Study

Invite someone to read the following text aloud:

Acts 13:1–4

Now in the church at Antioch there were prophets and teachers: Barnabas, Simeon who was called Niger, Lucius of Cyrene, Manaen a member of the court of Herod the ruler, and Saul. While they were worshiping the Lord and fasting, the Holy Spirit said, "Set apart for me Barnabas and Saul for the work to which I have called them." Then after fasting and praying they laid their hands on them and sent them off.

So, being sent out by the Holy Spirit, they went down to Seleucia; and from there they sailed to Cyprus.

For discussion

(1) The guidance provided by the Holy Spirit in this story came as the leaders of the church were worshiping together. Disciples of Christ defend an open table. Worship and communion are open to all with no theological or behavioral tests required other than our confession that Jesus is the Christ. Foundational to this discernment process about the gospel message to our church as we relate to lesbian and gay Christians is the commitment to worship together and to be open to the Holy Spirit in the midst of that worship. In your personal experience, what aspects of worship are most conducive to listening for new insight from God?

(2) The themes of praying, fasting, and listening to the Holy Spirit are all part of the spiritual disciplines of the faith experience for many Christians. Share personal stories or testimonies of your personal experiences of prayer and/or fasting as a way of listening to the Holy Spirit. What other spiritual disciplines do you employ in your listening for guidance?

Naming Our Fears and Prejudices

Have someone read the following statement aloud:

This stage involves naming our prejudices, our fears, and our commitments. Good discernment requires honesty and a willingness to engage in self-searching. For this discernment process to have integrity, each person must be allowed to express his or her honest thoughts and opinions and have those heard respectfully.

Remember that the rules for discernment are essential for the process to have integrity. Members of the group are asked to commit themselves to following these rules at each stage of the process.

1. I will honor and respect every participant as a person of faith.

2. I will claim a shared belief that the Holy Spirit is at work in the community.

3. I will examine scripture as a whole, not just isolated verses.

4. I will retain covenantal unity, an agreement to stay together in the process, even if there is no doctrinal unity.

5. Gay and lesbian persons must participate openly in order for the process to have integrity.

6. The church will be a safe and confidential place where people can discuss sensitive issues freely without feeling that they will be attacked or rejected.

Invite each person in the group to name his or her feelings about this covenant.

Watch the video of actors expressing a variety of approaches to the question of relating to gay and lesbian Christians. These vignettes are dramatizations, not the actual opinions of the actors.

Having seen this video, allow each person time to share her or his personal concerns, prejudices, and fears as you enter into the discernment process.

CLOSING WORSHIP

HYMN

COMMUNION

Words of Institution: 1 Corinthians 11:23–26
Prayer for the loaf and the cup
Partaking of the loaf and the cup

CLOSING PRAYER

BENEDICTION

As you depart, say to one another, "God be with you till we meet again."

Listening to Stories

In order to allow adequate time for the sharing of personal stories, you might want to divide this stage into two sessions, unless you happen to be in a retreat or other setting in which you have a large block of time. Remember that if you have two or more sessions in this stage, you should still open each one with worship and close each one with the Lord's supper.

OPENING WORSHIP

LITANY OF THE ONE SPIRIT

We call upon the Spirit of God to gather us together.
We honor the Spirit of God, dwelling in each of us.
We come to listen to one another.
And we come to listen for the Spirit who dwells within us all.
We honor this space as the place where God calls us together.
We cherish and protect what is shared in this space.
We find our unity in the One God, not in doctrine or argument.
We honor our unity in Christ.
To the One whom we honor and praise,
the One God who is Love. Amen.

INVOCATION (in unison)

O God, we have journeyed together to the place where listening is our watchword. You call us to listen

to your Word through scripture, to listen to how your Word has shaped each life of our traveling companions, and to listen for your Spirit to help us make sense of the interplay of our lives uniquely lived in devotion to you. Continue, we pray, to bless our shared journey in the simple and sacred act of the breaking of bread. Amen.

LIGHTING OF A CANDLE

God's Word is a lamp to our feet
and a light to our path.
We light this candle to remind us that we do not make this journey alone.
[Light candle here.]
May God light our way. Amen.

STATEMENT OF COVENANT

God, as facilitator of this discussion, invites us to enter into a covenant with God and with one another.
In response to God's invitation:
I will honor and respect every participant as a person of faith.
I will claim a shared belief that the Holy Spirit is present and at work in this community.
I will examine the whole of scripture, not just isolated verses.
I will earnestly seek to hear and understand perspectives different from my own.
I will seek to retain a unity of Spirit even when I disagree.
As God's church, this will be a safe and confidential place where people can discuss sensitive issues freely without feeling that they will be attacked or rejected. Amen.

PLACING OF THE WORSHIP SYMBOL

In this session you will be listening to personal stories. Add to the cross on your worship center a personal symbol that represents your lives and the stories about your lives that you will share. With the placing of your symbolic object, offer a sentence on why your group chose the symbol.

PART 1

Bible Study

No one is impartial in his or her reading and interpretation of scripture. Life experience and received teaching have informed the way each one sees, hears, and understands God's Word. As Christians, we study the Bible in community, not so that those in authority may define how others understand the texts, but so that the perspectives and insights of the community may inform and enlighten the whole body together. Until that day when we see the Christ face-to-face, we need one another, and we need to share the different "parts" we see. "For now we see in a mirror, dimly, but then we will see face to face. Now I know only in part; then I will know fully, even as I have been fully known" (1 Cor. 13:12).

Because all our conversations occur within a community of faith, it is incumbent on all of us to cultivate an appreciation for the mysterious ways that God still speaks and acts through the scriptures we share and to listen in humility to the stories of pain and joy our sisters and brothers in the faith have to tell. This will require us to accord a "good faith assumption" to one another from the very outset of our dialogue. As conversation partners in this process, we must begin with the assumption that we are equally serious about our commitment to the gospel of Jesus Christ and that we are mutually concerned about honoring the lordship of Jesus Christ in our settled convictions of faith and practice. Our heralded "unity in diversity" as a church depends in no small measure on our mutual respect for the freedom of faith we grant to one another to work out the implications of Christ's lordship in our own lives.

Theologian Karl Barth had little patience for theologians whose ideas differed from his own. Passionate about his beliefs, Barth could be difficult and obstinate in theological debate. And yet he was still compelled to admit, "I myself, together with my theological work, belong to the Christian Church solely on the basis of forgiveness, [and so] I have no right to deny or even to doubt that they [other theologians] were as fundamentally concerned as I am about the Christian faith."[3]

We must consciously make the same concession to one another, especially when we find ourselves disagreeing on important matters of faith and practice. Our spiritual heritage has never insisted that we agree with one another, but it has always insisted that we all be given the same chance to share deeply from our hearts on matters of conscience and that we treat each other gently and respectfully even in our disagreements. This is about

---

[3]Karl Barth, *Protestant Thought from Rousseau to Ritschl,* trans. Brian Cozens (New York: Simon and Schuster, 1959), 8.

more than civility for us; it's about conviction. So we now invite the sharing of personal stories within the context of the study of the following scriptures.

Invite someone to read the following text aloud:

Galatians 3:23–29

Now before faith came, we were imprisoned and guarded under the law until faith would be revealed. Therefore the law was our disciplinarian until Christ came, so that we might be justified by faith. But now that faith has come, we are no longer subject to a disciplinarian, for in Christ Jesus you are all children of God through faith. As many of you as were baptized into Christ have clothed yourselves with Christ. There is no longer Jew or Greek, there is no longer slave or free, there is no longer male and female; for all of you are one in Christ Jesus. And if you belong to Christ, then you are Abraham's offspring, heirs according to the promise.

For discussion

(1) Paul names various distinctions that used to define the social and religious life of Christians. What does he name as former distinctions? What, according to Paul, has ended these distinctions?

(2) You are invited to share briefly a transition or transformation story that is part of your faith journey with God in Christ Jesus. In what way have you changed in your Christian life?

PART 2

Watch videos of five members of the steering committee giving their personal testimonies.

Bible Study

Invite someone to read the following text aloud:

1 Corinthians 12:12–26

[12]For just as the body is one and has many members, and all the members of the body, though many, are one body, so it is with Christ. [13]For in the one Spirit we were all baptized into one body–Jews or Greeks, slaves or free–and we were all made to drink of one Spirit.

14Indeed, the body does not consist of one member but of many. 15If the foot would say, "Because I am not a hand, I do not belong to the body," that would not make it any less a part of the body. 16And if the ear would say, "Because I am not an eye, I do not belong to the body," that would not make it any less a part of the body. 17If the whole body were an eye, where would the hearing be? If the whole body were hearing, where would the sense of smell be? 18But as it is, God arranged the members in the body, each one of them, as he chose. 19If all were a single member, where would the body be? 20As it is, there are many members, yet one body. 21The eye cannot say to the hand, "I have no need of you," nor again the head to the feet, "I have no need of you." 22On the contrary, the members of the body that seem to be weaker are indispensable, 23and those members of the body that we think less honorable we clothe with greater honor, and our less respectable members are treated with greater respect; 24whereas our more respectable members do not need this. But God has so arranged the body, giving the greater honor to the inferior member, 25that there may be no dissension within the body, but the members may have the same care for one another. 26If one member suffers, all suffer together with it; if one member is honored, all rejoice together with it.

For discussion

(1) This text, among other things, speaks to the inherent unity of the body of Christ, the church. For Paul, what creates and sustains the unity of the body?

(2) Invite each person present to share a story about how she or he has related to persons who are lesbian or gay or has experienced life as a lesbian or gay person. [Remember that the guidelines for this discernment process include the expectation that the voices of openly lesbian and gay persons will be included in this time of story sharing.]

(3) After everyone has had a turn, enter into a few minutes of silence. Ask yourself, "What do I hear the Holy Spirit saying through these stories?"

CLOSING WORSHIP

HYMN

COMMUNION SERVICE

1 Corinthians 12:12–26 invites a celebration of each member of the body. Allow time at the conclusion of the Bible study to affirm the diversity and blessings of the whole body by celebrating each group member one at a time as she or he recites the following.

Member: "My name is _____.

I have been created to drink of the one Holy Spirit of God.

I am a valuable member of the body of Christ."

Group: "Thanks be to God for the gift of _____, an honored member of the body of Christ!"

[After each affirmation, allow fifteen to twenty seconds of silence as everyone breathes in, receiving afresh the Holy Spirit of God.]

Words of Institution: 1 Corinthians 11:23–26
Prayer for the loaf and the cup
Partaking of the loaf and the cup

CLOSING PRAYER

BENEDICTION

As you depart, say to one another, "God be with you till we meet again."

Bible Study of Texts Addressing Homosexuality

This stage includes a large number of texts to be studied, more than could possibly be worked through in one session. You will need to decide now many sessions to devote to this stage. The texts are grouped under five headings. The grouping may lend itself to five sessions, but you might have an extended session in a retreat or some other setting.

This is an appropriate time to review the principles of biblical interpretation found in stage 1. While you may have studied these passages before, take a new look at them now as if you had never seen them before.

However you may decide to divide this stage, remember that each session should begin with worship and end with communion

OPENING WORSHIP

LITANY OF THE ONE SPIRIT

We call upon the Spirit of God to gather us together.
We honor the Spirit of God, dwelling in each of us.
We come to listen to one another.
And we come to listen for the Spirit who dwells within us all.
We honor this space as the place where God calls us together.
We cherish and protect what is shared in this space.
We find our unity in the One God, not in doctrine or argument.
We honor our unity in Christ.

To the One whom we honor and praise,
the One God who is Love. Amen.

INVOCATION (in unison)

O God, we have traveled far enough together now to know the path ahead is strewn with possibilities and pain. We face the possibilities of the thrill of new gospel discovery and the pain of discovering our personal distance from your truth. We call upon your Spirit to sustain us, enlighten us, and unite us as we grow in our awareness that all your journeys are made in the shadow of your cross. Continue, we pray, to bless our shared journey in the simple and sacred act of the breaking of bread. Amen.

LIGHTING OF A CANDLE

God's Word is a lamp to our feet
and a light to our path.
We light this candle to remind us that we do not make this journey alone.
[Light candle here.]
May God light our way. Amen.

STATEMENT OF COVENANT

God, as facilitator of this discussion, invites us to enter into a covenant with God and with one another.
In response to God's invitation:
I will honor and respect every participant as a person of faith.
I will claim a shared belief that the Holy Spirit is present and at work in this community.
I will examine the whole of scripture, not just isolated verses.
I will earnestly seek to hear and understand perspectives different from my own.
I will seek to retain a unity of Spirit even when I disagree.
As God's church, this will be a safe and confidential place where people can discuss sensitive issues freely without feeling that they will be attacked or rejected. Amen.

PLACING OF THE WORSHIP SYMBOL

Scripture reminds us that God's Word is a lamp to our feet. We add a Bible to the cross and personal symbols on our worship center.

Bible Study

This stage involves a careful study of the biblical passages that have been understood as addressing homosexuality, as well as others pertinent to this discernment process. You will be presented with theological perspectives that illustrate the complexity and range of biblical interpretation.

Before beginning your study, watch the video of the committee studying the question, Is homosexuality a sin?

Preface to the Bible Studies in Stage 4

Biblically informed discussion about lesbian and gay Christians in the life of the church has frequently focused on a set of specific texts understood by many to reference homosexual behavior. Others dispute the appropriateness of applying ancient texts about abusive or idolatrous relationships to the loving, committed relationships of many lesbian and gay persons.

Our spiritual tradition has characteristically weighed the whole counsel of God when deciding matters of faith and practice rather than depending on isolated proof-texts. Yet because these texts are almost always cited in this conversation, we do well to identify and discuss such texts in this discernment process, with the understanding that these do not define the limits of our conversations.

The fact is, the cultural chasm between biblical times and ours precludes our being able to make direct correlations between whatever behavior is being referenced in some of these biblical texts and the moral/spiritual realities of Christians today. And the issues at stake about our understanding of God and the church are much more complicated than the concerns these texts address. Questions such as "What is the nature of the church and of our covenantal relationship with one another as Christians, congregations, regions, and general manifestations of the church?" and "What guidelines define healthy and holy intimate relationships for Christians and other people of good faith?" may be prerequisite conversations for adequate consideration of the church's relationship to lesbian and gay Christians.

The following studies consider texts (or sets of texts) that, as part of the biblical canon, will inform our conversation, but that in the end cannot be determinative in themselves. The received testimony of God's will and ways are much larger than these few texts.

PART 1: Inhospitality and Sexual Violence

Most scholars now readily concede that the following text is not about homosexuality but about a breach in the practice of hospitality that could result in rape and that rape is not about sex but about power.

Invite someone to read the following text aloud:

Genesis 19:1–11

¹The two angels came to Sodom in the evening, and Lot was sitting in the gateway of Sodom. When Lot saw them, he rose to meet them, and bowed down with his face to the ground. ²He said, "Please, my lords, turn aside to your servant's house and spend the night, and wash your feet; then you can rise early and go on your way." They said, "No; we will spend the night in the square." ³But he urged them strongly; so they turned aside to him and entered his house; and he made them a feast, and baked unleavened bread, and they ate.

⁴But before they lay down, the men of the city, the men of Sodom, both young and old, all the people to the last man, surrounded the house; ⁵and they called to Lot, "Where are the men who came to you tonight? Bring them out to us, so that we may know them." ⁶Lot went out of the door to the men, shut the door after him, ⁷and said, "I beg you, my brothers, do not act so wickedly. ⁸Look, I have two daughters who have not known a man; let me bring them out to you, and do to them as you please; only do nothing to these men, for they have come under the shelter of my roof." ⁹But they replied, "Stand back!" And they said, "This fellow came here as an alien, and he would play the judge! Now we will deal worse with you than with them." Then they pressed hard against the man Lot, and came near the door to break it down. ¹⁰But the men inside reached out their hands and brought Lot into the house with them, and shut the door. ¹¹And they struck with blindness the men who were at the door of the house, both small and great, so that they were unable to find the door.

For discussion

(1) The ancient Near East principle of hospitality required absolute respect for and care of the stranger (alien). To refuse gracious hospitality to any stranger incurred the worst of God's wrath (Ex. 22:21–24; Lev. 19:33–34; Deut. 10:19; Heb. 13:2).

Read aloud Genesis 18:1–16 and discuss the principle of hospitality at work in Abraham's reception of these men (angels?) from God.

(2) Read Genesis 18:16–22 and 19:1–11 aloud from at least two different translations. Read the text aloud while walking around so that your body, mind, and spirit are free to experience the text as well as hear it.

(3) Compare the story of Abraham's showing hospitality (Gen. 18) to Lot's desire to provide hospitality to the angels. Do you think that Lot knew that the men were angels? (Jude 6–7 implies that the men of the city knew that Lot's guests were angels. (Compare Gen. 6:1–8.) What acts of hospitality does Lot offer?

(4) How are we to hear God's counsel in this text as it may relate to women and to the rape of women? (Compare and contrast this story with the story told in Judges 19:22–30.)

(5) Examine how Sodom and Gomorrah are discussed in other biblical texts. How is the sin of Sodom defined and in what context? (Ezek. 16:48–50; Mt. 10:5–15 / Lk. 10:3–12; Jude 7)

(6) It seems quite clear that the men of the city intended acts of sexual violence against the guests in Lot's house. Do you think we are to understand that *every* man in the city was homosexual? What point do you think is being made by this detail of the story? Why do you think this story about an intended gang rape has been used to justify the condemnation of loving same-gender relationships?

(7) For a greater understanding of the text recreate as a group the drama of the story. Act it out. Then discuss your feelings from the perspective of the character you portrayed. Finally, allow time for silent prayer and reflection. Listen for the Spirit's teaching in the midst of this experience. Discuss.

(8) Name the principles of biblical interpretation that inform your present understanding of this text. (See pages 20–21 of this resource.)

PART 2: Holiness and Purity

Knowledge of culture and context gives clues to understanding the significance of any text, ancient or modern. The "Holiness Code" or purity codes of ancient Israel provide the context for certain texts used by many to condemn bisexual, lesbian, gay, and transgendered relationships today.

Read the texts. It may be useful to assign the reading of Leviticus 17–26 before the group gathers for community study of the texts. Ideally, everyone will read all ten chapters of these holiness codes, which set forth the conditions by which the people of Israel would define purity—that is, what makes someone or something clean or unclean, with unclean being defined as sinful. If reading the entire holiness code is too daunting, we ask that the group read aloud Leviticus 19 in its entirety to get a feel for the range of concerns these laws address.

For discussion

Having read Leviticus 17 through 26, the "Holiness Code" or purity code of Israel, make notes about all the ways one can become unclean. Which rules are for priests? Which for men? Which for women? Why do you think the distinction is made? Which of these laws do you consider to be valid today? On what basis do we exempt ourselves or others from some purity laws (such as mixing dairy and meat products in meals or different fibers in our clothes) and insist on obedience to others?

Invite someone to read the following texts aloud:

Leviticus 18:22, 20:13

You shall not lie with a male as with a woman; it is an abomination (Lev. 18:22) .

If a man lies with a male as with a woman, both of them have committed an abomination; they shall be put to death; their blood is upon them (Lev. 20:13).

For discussion

Specifically look at Leviticus 18:22 and 20:13. What principles of biblical interpretation do you apply to these verses? Why do you think that only men are mentioned and not women? Note: Nothing in Jewish law explicitly forbids or condemns sexual intercourse between women. What is the relationship of these verses to other purity laws in this section of Leviticus?

Holiness and Purity in the Jesus Tradition

Based on recent study of the New Testament, we understand that the ministry of Jesus included a corrective to the extremes of the purity system of the Jewish social world of the first century. At the same time, it is clear that Jesus did not propose anarchy or moral license. Instead, he invites a return to the heart of the law, to the law of love and of responsibility to the community.

Invite someone to read the following texts aloud:

Matthew 23:23 (Cf. Lk. 11:37–42)

"Woe to you, scribes and Pharisees, hypocrites! For you tithe mint, dill, and cummin, and have neglected the weightier matters of the law: justice and mercy and faith. It is these you ought to have practiced without neglecting the others."

Matthew 22:36–40 (Cf. Mk. 12:28–31; Lk. 10:25–37)

"Teacher, which commandment in the law is the greatest?" He said to him, "'You shall love the Lord your God with all your heart, and with all your soul, and with all your mind.' This is the greatest and first commandment. And a second is like it: 'You shall love your neighbor as yourself.' On these two commandments hang all the law and the prophets."

For discussion

(1) The early church continued to struggle with the balance between holiness/purity and love/grace. How do the two texts above address that difficult balance?

(2) With the context of the purity codes of Israel in mind, read Luke 10:25–37, the parable of the good Samaritan (which Luke uses to illustrate the great commandment). Discuss how difficult this story must have been for Jewish ears to hear.

(3) Different New Testament texts reflect different senses of the balance between the truths of holiness/purity and love/grace. The compassionate inclusion found in stories such as the parable of the good Samaritan are set alongside stories reporting exclusion, such as the parable of Lazarus and the rich man (Lk. 16:19–31). How do you live with the tension between Christ's example and exhortation to compassion and Christ's demand for righteousness and personal transformation?

(4) Together examine and discuss other New Testament texts that demonstrate principles used by Jesus and the church to move beyond a purity definition of faithfulness and justice. (For example: Mt. 15:1–11; Mk. 1:40–45; 5:21–34; Lk. 7:36–50.) Discuss how the gospel accounts of Jesus' teaching and living reflect the process of the early church and inform the discernment process of our church today.

PART 3: Vice Lists and Christian Behavior

The early church lived out its faith trying to balance Christ's example and exhortation to inclusive love with Christ's demand for righteousness and personal transformation in the midst of an often hostile world. The New Testament's "vice lists" were one of the tools used in this process. Vice lists were commonly used in the first century as a way to speak ill of a person or group in the context of persuading an audience to avoid "them" and join "us." In 1 Corinthians 6:9–11, Paul uses a vice list to celebrate the difference Christ makes in someone's life. Here are three examples of vice lists in the New Testament.

Invite someone to read the following texts aloud:

1 Corinthians 6:9–10

Do you not know that wrongdoers will not inherit the kingdom of God? Do not be deceived! Fornicators, idolaters, adulterers, male prostitutes, sodomites, thieves, the greedy, drunkards, revilers, robbers—none of these will inherit the kingdom of God.

Galatians 5:19–21

Now the works of the flesh are obvious: fornication, impurity, licentiousness, idolatry, sorcery, enmities, strife, jealousy, anger, quarrels, dissensions, factions, envy, drunkenness, carousing, and things like these. I am warning you, as I warned you before: those who do such things will not inherit the kingdom of God.

2 Timothy 3:2–5

For people will be lovers of themselves, lovers of money, boasters, arrogant, abusive, disobedient to their parents, ungrateful, unholy, inhuman, implacable, slanderers, profligates, brutes, haters of good, treacherous, reckless, swollen with conceit, lovers of pleasure rather than lovers of God, holding to the outward form of godliness but denying its power. Avoid them!

For discussion

(1) Compare and contrast the lists. Which vices occur in each list? Which vices occur in one list only? Read the chapter in which each list is found. How does each list function in its

context? What is your assessment of the success of Paul's use of the vice list to make his point?

(2) The biblical expectation is that each person will use these lists as mirrors, inviting self-evaluation, confession, and transformation. Where do you see yourself in these lists? What happens when we use a vice list to judge others?

(3) The Bible has an egalitarian view of sin. As Romans 3:23 says, "All have sinned and fall short of the glory of God." Discuss: "Vice lists may contribute to a smug self-righteousness among some, but they are supposed to serve the sanctification of all."

Culture, Translation, and Interpretation

Sometimes we forget that the majority of North American Christians read the Bible in English translation, not in the original languages in which they were written. Likewise, having heard the biblical stories over and over again, we forget about the wide chasm between the first-century Near-Eastern cultures and our own twenty-first-century realities.

Read 1 Corinthians 6:9–10 in as many different translations as you can find. What one or two words follow the word *adulterers* and precede the word *thieves* in the various translations? These words are attempts to translate the Greek words *malakoi* and *arsenokoitai*. Make a chart in order to compare the translations. Here are four more English translations of 1 Corinthians 6:9–10 to add to the *New Revised Standard Version* and others you may have available.

1 Corinthians 6:9–10

King James Version	Know ye not that the unrighteous shall not inherit the kingdom of God? Be not deceived: neither fornicators, nor idolaters, nor adulterers, **nor effeminate, nor abusers of themselves with mankind**, nor thieves, nor covetous, nor drunkards, nor revilers, nor extortioners, shall inherit the kingdom of God.
J. B. Phillips	Have you forgotten that the kingdom of God will never belong to the wicked? Don't be under any illusion, neither the impure, the idolater or the adulterer; **neither the effeminate, the pervert** or the thief; neither the swindler, the drunkard, the foul-mouthed or the rapacious shall have any share in the kingdom of God.

New International Version	Do you not know that the wicked will not inherit the kingdom of God? Do not be deceived: Neither the sexually immoral nor idolaters nor adulterers **nor male prostitutes nor homosexual offenders** nor thieves nor the greedy nor drunkards nor slanderers nor swindlers will inherit the kingdom of God.
Living Bible (paraphrase)	Don't you know that those who do such things have no share in the king dom of God? Don't fool yourselves. Those who live immoral lives, who are idol worshippers, adulterers or **homosexuals** will have no share in His kingdom. Neither will thieves or greedy people, drunkards, slander mongers, or robbers.

For discussion

(1) What is wrong with this picture? Remember that the concept and word *homosexuality* did not exist until the late nineteenth century. The idea of a homosexual person as one who is, by nature, exclusively or predominantly attracted to members of the same sex seems to have been unknown to the ancient world. A danger lies in identifying modern terms with ancient realities. Without a clear understanding of the "wrong relationships" obviously referenced by Paul in a culture very different from today, translators run the risk of presenting a contemporary "interpretation" as an accurate "translation," thus misrepresenting the meaning for today. The truth is, scholars do not know exactly what the terms *malakoi* and *arsenokoitai* referenced. Ideological interests in marginalizing homosexual persons have influenced some of these translations as much as have generally accepted principles of biblical interpretation. For example, note the emphasis implied by placing "will have no share in the kingdom" immediately after "homosexuals" in the *Living Bible* paraphrase.

(2) How do you feel about knowing that English translations can be biased and even inaccurate? Short of learning the biblical languages, what safeguards are available to people who want to understand the scriptures as faithfully as possible?

PART 4: Intimacy and Family

Is there a New Testament "norm" for families? Yes. Jesus, who, contrary to expectations for rabbis, was apparently not married, makes a radical claim to supersede all former definitions of family, basing his norm on discipleship, on hearing and doing God's will (Mt. 12:46–50; Mk. 3:31–35; Lk. 8:19–21).

Mark 3:31–35

31Then his mother and his brothers came; and standing outside, they sent to him and called him. 32A crowd was sitting around him; and they said to him, "Your mother and your brothers and sisters are outside, asking for you." 33And he replied, "Who are my mother and my brothers?" 34And looking at those who sat around him, he said, "Here are my mother and my brothers! 35Whoever does the will of God is my brother and sister and mother."

The Bible offers a wide range of stories of intimate and/or sexual relationships. The texts about relationships between one man and one woman are generally understood as the norm and have been emphasized in our preaching and teaching (Heb. 13:4; Mk. 10:2–9; 1 Thess. 4:3–8). Accounts presented without critique about polygamous relationships, such as that of Abraham/Sarah /Hagar are generally avoided in moral discussions. The early church's position that celibacy is the preferred status (1 Cor. 7:1–9) is dismissed by most, in light of its sociohistorical context. We know that many thought that the return of Christ was so imminent that marriage would only distract from preparedness for the end.

Many examples of intimate and affectionate same-gender relationships are described in scripture. We do not need to believe that these relationships were sexual to note that these texts bear positive witness to loving, committed same-gender friendships. In fact, these relationships of intimacy and affection (Prov. 18:24) are biblical norms for all our relationships. When we consider loving gay and lesbian relationships, many note that these scriptures should inform our thinking more than texts that speak of sexual violence.

The cherished expression of human love, and a favorite text at weddings, "Where you go, I will go; Where you lodge, I will lodge; your people shall be my people, and your God my God. Where you die, I will die—there will I be buried" (Ruth 1:16–17), was spoken by one woman to another. First Samuel 18:1–5; 19:1; 20:1–42 tells the story of the very special friendship between David and Jonathan. When Jonathan dies, David weeps, professing that "greatly beloved were you to me; your love to me was wonderful, passing the love of women" (2 Sam. 1:26). And the gospel of John refers to "the disciple whom Jesus loved," who lay his head on Jesus' breast (John 21:7, 20).

For discussion

(1) Survey the scriptures to list the various kinds of family/intimate relationships presented. Identify those presented (a) without comment, (b) with approval, (c) with condemnation, (d) with different assessments at different times.

(Gen. 2:18–25; 16:1–6; 29:15–30; Ruth 1:15–18; 4:7–17; 2 Sam. 11; 20; 2 Sam. 2:25–26; 1 Kings 11:1–8; Hos. 1:1–9; Jn. 19:26–27; Acts 18:18–28, etc.)

(2) Make a list of the various family configurations within your church and community. In what ways have acceptance of these families changed?

(3) Note what principles of biblical interpretation influence your openness to each family type, both biblical and contemporary.

Part 5: Nature, Sin, and Gospel

Paul begins to support his thesis that the gospel "is the power of God for salvation to everyone who has faith" (Rom. 1:16) by establishing everyone's need for the kind of salvation that the gospel of Jesus Christ provides. Romans 1:18–2:20 establishes Paul's egalitarian view of sin: "All have sinned and fall short of the glory of God" (3:23). The argument is bracketed by universal declarations of our fallenness—the "all" of Romans 1:18 matched by the "all" of Romans 3:9. Between these two "alls" the particular indictment of Gentiles and Jews is made according to the differing knowledge of God they each possess: Gentiles by general revelation in creation and conscience and Jews by special revelation in the Law. A responsible reading of Paul's argument recognizes that the shameless acts castigated in Romans 1:26–27 are examples of the many sins listed by Paul in Romans 1:24–32 as evidence of our general sinfulness as human beings. Surely Paul intended for all of us to find ourselves unmistakably and frequently in his argument. The circle Paul draws encompasses us all.

Invite someone to read the following text aloud:

Romans 1:16–2:11

16For I am not ashamed of the gospel; it is the power of God for salvation to everyone who has faith, to the Jew first and also to the Greek. [17]For in it the righteousness of God is revealed through faith for faith; as it is written, "The one who is righteous will live by faith."

[18]For the wrath of God is revealed from heaven against all ungodliness and wickedness of those who by their wickedness suppress the truth. [19]For what can be known about God is plain to them, because God has shown it to them. [20]Ever since the creation of the world God's eternal power and divine nature, invisible though they are, have been understood and seen through the things God has made. So they are without excuse; [21]for though they knew God, they did not honor God as God or give thanks to God, but they became futile in their thinking, and their senseless minds were darkened. [22]Claiming to be wise, they became fools; [23]and they exchanged the glory of the immortal God for images resembling a mortal human being or birds or four-footed animals or reptiles.

[24]Therefore God gave them up in the lusts of their hearts to impurity, to the degrading of their bodies among themselves, [25]because they exchanged the truth about God for a lie and worshiped and served the creature rather than the Creator, who is blessed forever! Amen.

[26]For this reason God gave them up to degrading passions. Their women exchanged natural intercourse for unnatural, [27]and in the same way also the men, giving up natural intercourse with women, were consumed with passion for one another. Men committed shameless acts with men and received in their own persons the due penalty for their error.

[28]And since they did not see fit to acknowledge God, God gave them up to a debased mind and to things that should not be done. [29]They were filled with every kind of wickedness, evil, covetousness, malice. Full of envy, murder, strife, deceit, craftiness, they are gossips, [30]slanderers, God-haters, insolent, haughty, boastful, inventors of evil, rebellious toward parents, [31]foolish, faithless, heartless, ruthless. [32]They know God's decree, that those who practice such things deserve to die— yet they not only do them but even applaud others who practice them.

2:1 Therefore you have no excuse, whoever you are, when you judge others; for in passing judgment on another you condemn yourself, because you, the judge, are doing the very same things. [2]You say, "We know that God's judgment on those who do such things is in accordance with truth." [3]Do you imagine, whoever you are, that when you judge those who do such things and yet do them yourself, you will escape the judgment of God? [4]Or do you despise the riches of God's kindness and forbearance and patience? Do you not realize that God's kindness is meant to lead you to repentance? [5]But by your hard and impenitent heart you are storing up wrath for yourself on the day of wrath, when God's righteous judgment will be revealed. [6]For God will repay according to each one's deeds: [7]to those who by patiently doing good seek for glory and honor and immortality, he will give eternal life; [8]while for those who are self-seeking and who obey not the truth but wickedness, there will be wrath and fury. [9]There will be anguish and distress for everyone who does evil, the Jew first and also the Greek, [10]but glory and honor and peace for everyone who does good, the Jew first and also the Greek. [11]For God shows no partiality.

For discussion

(1) As each is able, all members of the group read Romans 1:16–2:11 aloud and at the same time, while walking or moving around the room. Read aloud at your own pace, opening yourself to the movement of the text and the passion of the message. Discuss: What new insights appeared as you experienced the text this way? What point does Paul argue in this passage? What verse do you think summarizes Paul's message? Explain your choice.

(2) Disagreements abound about appropriate principles of biblical interpretation for understanding this text with respect to its references to same-gender sex: (a) Some exegetes say that the text clearly condemns homosexual behavior. End of discussion. (b) Some exegetes note the way Paul designs this passage. He begins by listing culturally agreed-upon offenses, eliciting a judgmental attitude from the hearers, thereby catching everyone in the just condemnation of God (Rom. 2:1), in order to demonstrate the need for God's mercy for all. (c) Some exegetes focus on Paul's definition of what is "natural," noting that Paul and others in his culture assumed that all people were "naturally" heterosexual, so that homosexual acts were a distortion of God's intention. Modern

science and sociology now understand a homosexual orientation to be "natural" for persons who are lesbian or gay. Indeed, sexual intimacy with the *opposite* sex may be a distortion of God's intention for lesbian and gay persons. How does understanding "natural" in this way change the interpretation of Paul's illustration?

(3) Share and compare with one another your experiences of what feelings and desires are "natural" and how you first came to the awareness of what is "natural" for you. What kind of internal consequences might result if you were to go against that which is your God-given nature? Invite the testimonies of several lesbian or gay Christians, listening for their experiences of what feelings and desires are "natural." Listen to each person's story of salvation received by the grace of God in Christ Jesus as it relates to his or her understanding of his or her sexual nature.

Afterword to Stage 4 Bible Studies

The struggle between holiness and love is at the very heart of scripture, and how we sort it out will directly affect our understanding of sin, grace, and righteousness. From various theological positions, what is at stake here is the integrity of the gospel we preach and believe.

- Is the essential core of the gospel a message about the all-inclusive love of God as demonstrated in the life, death, and resurrection of Jesus the Christ?

- Is the essential core of the gospel a message about the opposition of a holy God to anything contrary to God's purposes as heard in the rigorous demands for repentance and discipleship made by Jesus the Christ?

Each of us has the responsibility for taking what the scriptures say about God's holiness and God's love and allowing ourselves to be transformed as the gospel becomes real for us. As Disciples of Christ we cherish our tradition of theological freedom that allows no creed but Christ, and we refuse the attempt of any to seize the authority and power to define the gospel for all. The question is, and always has been for our church, how will we live and work together in the same community of faith when our understandings of the gospel have different emphases on holiness and love?

Discuss how our covenant to remain in fellowship with one another in the midst of differing understandings of the work of Christ can be applied in the midst of this discernment process about the gospel message to our church as we relate to lesbian and gay Christians?

CLOSING WORSHIP

HYMN

COMMUNION

> Words of Institution: 1 Corinthians 11:23–26
> Prayer for the loaf and the cup
> Partaking of the loaf and the cup

CLOSING PRAYER

BENEDICTION

As you depart, say to one another, "God be with you till we meet again."

What Has Happened to Me Personally, and What Has God Called Me to Do?

OPENING WORSHIP

LITANY OF THE ONE SPIRIT

We call upon the Spirit of God to gather us together.
We honor the Spirit of God, dwelling in each of us.
We come to listen to one another.
And we come to listen for the Spirit who dwells within us all.
We honor this space as the place where God calls us together.
We cherish and protect what is shared in this space.
We find our unity in the One God, not in doctrine or argument.
We honor our unity in Christ.
To the One whom we honor and praise,
the One God who is Love. Amen.

INVOCATION (in unison)

O God, we have traveled a long way together. The road has not been easy. We have heard many voices: yours, O Lord, one another's, and our own. We call upon your Spirit and the gentle, discerning spirit of one another to make sense of what we have heard. Open us even further to the Spirit of truth, we pray. Grant us the ability to accept its lure of embrace. Chart the course you would have us walk from this

day forth. Continue, we pray, to bless our shared
journey in the simple and sacred act of the breaking
of bread. Amen.

LIGHTING OF A CANDLE

God's Word is a lamp to our feet
and a light to our path.
We light this candle to remind us that we do not make this
journey alone.
[Light candle here.]
May God light our way. Amen.

STATEMENT OF COVENANT

God, as facilitator of this discussion, invites us to enter into a
covenant with God and with one another.
In response to God's invitation:
**I will honor and respect every participant as a person of
faith.**
**I will claim a shared belief that the Holy Spirit is present and
at work in this community.**
I will examine the whole of scripture, not just isolated verses.
**I will earnestly seek to hear and understand perspectives
different from my own.**
I will seek to retain a unity of Spirit even when I disagree.
**As God's church, this will be a safe and confidential place
where people can discuss sensitive issues freely without
feeling that they will be attacked or rejected. Amen.**

*[Note: The placing of the worship symbol will be done during the
closing worship of this session.]*

Bible Study

Invite someone to read the following text aloud:

Luke 10:25–37

25Just then a lawyer stood up to test Jesus. "Teacher," he said,
"what must I do to inherit eternal life?" 26He said to him,
"What is written in the law? What do you read there?" 27He
answered, "You shall love the Lord your God with all your
heart, and with all your soul, and with all your strength, and
with all your mind; and your neighbor as yourself." 28And
he said to him, "You have given the right answer; do this,
and you will live."

^{29}But wanting to justify himself, he asked Jesus, "And who is my neighbor?" ^{30}Jesus replied, "A man was going down from Jerusalem to Jericho, and fell into the hands of robbers, who stripped him, beat him, and went away, leaving him half dead. ^{31}Now by chance a priest was going down that road; and when he saw him, he passed by on the other side. ^{32}So likewise a Levite, when he came to the place and saw him, passed by on the other side. ^{33}But a Samaritan while traveling came near him; and when he saw him, he was moved with pity. ^{34}He went to him and bandaged his wounds, having poured oil and wine on them. Then he put him on his own animal, brought him to an inn, and took care of him. ^{35}The next day he took out two denarii, gave them to the innkeeper, and said, 'Take care of him; and when I come back, I will repay you whatever more you spend.' ^{36}Which of these three, do you think, was a neighbor to the man who fell into the hands of the robbers?" ^{37}He said, "The one who showed him mercy." Jesus said to him, "Go and do likewise."

For discussion

(1) Why did the priest and the Levite avoid the man who had fallen into the hands of robbers? Consider the laws about cleanliness and holiness in Leviticus 21:1–22:9 and discuss how difficult this story must have been for Jewish ears to hear. What would constitute an equally offensive and challenging illustration for the church today?

(2) The lawyer stands up to ask, "And who is my neighbor?" Jesus' response was this story followed by the question about who "neighbored" the man who fell into the hands of robbers. What do you know about the relationship between Jews and Samaritans? Why did Jews avoid Samaritans? What, do you think, was Jesus calling the lawyer and others who heard this story to do?

(3) What is the relationship between biblical law and gospel mandate in this text? How does this gospel passage speak to our church's discernment process?

(4) Invite each participant in this study to a time of personal reflection during which each one answers the questions, What has happened to me personally as we have studied and prayed and shared stories about persons in the church who are lesbian or gay? What does God call me to do? Provide

paper, pencils, crayons, glue stick, scissors, modeling clay, and so forth, for the group. Each person should answer these questions using the supplies provided. Set aside at least fifteen minutes for personal prayer, journaling, and/or creative art reflection—something that represents an "aha" moment for each member as a result of this process.

(5) Divide into groups of two or three and invite each person to share his or her insights from the time of personal prayer, journaling, and/or art reflection.

(6) As a group, discuss what has happened in your congregation. Together consider what God is calling your congregation to do.

CLOSING WORSHIP

HYMN

COMMUNION SERVICE

Words of Institution: 1 Corinthians 11:23–26
Prayer for the loaf and the cup
Partaking of the loaf and the cup

OFFERING

Each person places the object made or writing done in question 4 on the worship center and makes a brief statement about the meaning of the symbol.

OFFERING PRAYER

O God, you have blessed us with new insights into your Word and deepened our relationship with you and with one another. We offer to you these symbols of our becoming new creations in Christ. Bless our lives and our journey, we pray. Amen.

CLOSING PRAYER

BENEDICTION

As you depart, say to one another, "God be with you till we meet again."

What Is the Next Step?

OPENING WORSHIP

LITANY OF THE ONE SPIRIT

We call upon the Spirit of God to gather us together.
We honor the Spirit of God, dwelling in each of us.
We come to listen to one another.
And we come to listen for the Spirit who dwells within us all.
We honor this space as the place where God calls us together.
We cherish and protect what is shared in this space.
We find our unity in the One God, not in doctrine or argument.
We honor our unity in Christ.
To the One whom we honor and praise,
the One God who is Love. Amen.

INVOCATION (in unison)

O God, our prayer now comes in the form of a question, Where do we go from here? Show us the way as we unite hearts, minds, and spirits in your Spirit and celebrate our oneness in the breaking of the bread. Amen.

LIGHTING OF A CANDLE

God's Word is a lamp to our feet
and a light to our path.

We light this candle to remind us that we do not make this journey alone.

[Light candle here.]

May God light our way. Amen.

STATEMENT OF COVENANT

God, as facilitator of this discussion, invites us to enter into a covenant with God and with one another.

In response to God's invitation:

I will honor and respect every participant as a person of faith.

I will claim a shared belief that the Holy Spirit is present and at work in this community.

I will examine the whole of scripture, not just isolated verses.

I will earnestly seek to hear and understand perspectives different from my own.

I will seek to retain a unity of Spirit even when I disagree.

As God's church, this will be a safe and confidential place where people can discuss sensitive issues freely without feeling that they will be attacked or rejected. Amen.

PLACING OF THE WORSHIP SYMBOL

We place a box of jigsaw puzzle pieces on the table to remind us of our interconnectedness with one another. It also reminds us that our relationship requires thoughtful efforts and willing spirits to come together as the body of Christ. The fact that each piece is different reminds us of our diversity.

Bible Study

In the middle of the first century, inclusion of uncircumcised believers in the church was a volatile and difficult concern for the leaders. Within the church were various groups. Some believers felt bound by Holy Scripture (our Old Testament) to hold fast to the condition that only those who were circumcised had access to the promises of God. Others, noting the experiences and testimonies of uncircumcised persons who became believers, insisted that, in Jesus Christ, faith alone was the criterion for inclusion in the church. Paul addresses the controversy over and over again in his undisputed letters. The struggle to honor the whole of scripture continues to this day as we seek to discern God's will for the church in our time, just as the first-century Christians did in their time. The witness of the New Testament is that the decision process happened in steps and that the process was interpreted differently by different people.

Invite someone or a group of persons to read the following text aloud:(Suggested readers: Narrator, Peter, James, Silas [letter])

Acts 15:1–29

¹Then certain individuals came down from Judea and were teaching the brothers, "Unless you are circumcised according to the custom of Moses, you cannot be saved." ²And after Paul and Barnabas had no small dissension and debate with them, Paul and Barnabas and some of the others were appointed to go up to Jerusalem to discuss this question with the apostles and the elders. ³So they were sent on their way by the church, and as they passed through both Phoenicia and Samaria, they reported the conversion of the Gentiles, and brought great joy to all the believers. ⁴When they came to Jerusalem, they were welcomed by the church and the apostles and the elders, and they reported all that God had done with them. ⁵But some believers who belonged to the sect of the Pharisees stood up and said, "It is necessary for them to be circumcised and ordered to keep the law of Moses."

⁶The apostles and the elders met together to consider this matter. ⁷After there had been much debate, Peter stood up and said to them, "My brothers, you know that in the early days God made a choice among you, that I should be the one through whom the Gentiles would hear the message of the good news and become believers. ⁸And God, who knows the human heart, testified to them by giving them the Holy Spirit, just as God did to us; ⁹and in cleansing their hearts by faith God has made no distinction between them and us. ¹⁰Now therefore why are you putting God to the test by placing on the neck of the disciples a yoke that neither our ancestors nor we have been able to bear? ¹¹On the contrary, we believe that we will be saved through the grace of the Lord Jesus, just as they will."

¹²The whole assembly kept silence, and listened to Barnabas and Paul as they told of all the signs and wonders that God had done through them among the Gentiles. ¹³After they finished speaking, James replied, "My brothers, listen to me.

[14]Simeon has related how God first looked favorably on the Gentiles, to take from among them a people for God's name. [15]This agrees with the words of the prophets, as it is written,

[16]'After this I will return, and I will rebuild the dwelling of David, which has fallen; from its ruins I will rebuild it, and I will set it up, [17]so that all other peoples may seek the Lord— even all the Gentiles over whom my name has been called. Thus says the Lord, who has been making these things [18]known from long ago.'

[19]Therefore I have reached the decision that we should not trouble those Gentiles who are turning to God, [20]but we should write to them to abstain only from things polluted by idols and from fornication and from whatever has been strangled and from blood. [21]For in every city, for generations past, Moses has had those who proclaim him, for he has been read aloud every sabbath in the synagogues."

[22]Then the apostles and the elders, with the consent of the whole church, decided to choose men from among their members and to send them to Antioch with Paul and Barnabas. They sent Judas called Barsabbas, and Silas, leaders among the brothers, [23]with the following letter:

"The brothers, both the apostles and the elders, to the believers of Gentile origin in Antioch and Syria and Cilicia, greetings. [24]Since we have heard that certain persons who have gone out from us, though with no instructions from us, have said things to disturb you and have unsettled your minds, [25]we have decided unanimously to choose representatives and send them to you, along with our beloved Barnabas and Paul, [26]who have risked their lives for the sake of our Lord Jesus Christ. [27]We have therefore sent Judas and Silas, who themselves will tell you the same things by word of mouth. [28]For it has seemed good to the Holy Spirit and to us to impose on you no further burden than these essentials: [29]that you abstain from what has been sacrificed to idols and from blood and from what is strangled and from fornication. If you keep yourselves from these, you will do well. Farewell."

For discussion

(1) According to this account in Acts, what was the position of the Judean believers regarding Gentiles before coming to the

Council at Jerusalem? (v. 1) What was the strategy of Paul and Barnabas on the way to the Council at Jerusalem? (vv. 3, 4) How does the Judean position shift in light of the testimonies about Gentile converts? (v. 5)

(2) Summarize the testimony of Peter. (vv. 7–11) What was the nature of the testimony of Paul and Barnabas? (v. 12)

(3) James, the leader of the church at Jerusalem, makes a unilateral decision, a decision based on scripture texts other than those that were being held up as the standard by the Judean believers. Discuss James' process and conclusions. (vv. 13–21)

(4) As members of the Christian Church (Disciples of Christ), we are not accustomed to expecting (or even allowing) powerful church leaders to make decisions for us. What do you see as the role of church leadership in this and other discernment processes of the church?

(5) The apostles, the elders, and the whole church concur with James and send a letter to the Gentile believers (vv. 23–29). Discuss this resolution in light of the earlier debate as reported in Acts.

(6) Note and discuss the nature of scriptural authority for the different groups and persons involved in this account of the early church's struggle to discern the will of God in the midst of clear differences of opinion.

Another View

Many scholars understand Galatians 2:1–10 to be Paul's account of the Council at Jerusalem described by Luke in Acts 15. Some scholars, noting the differences in the details of the two accounts, argue that Paul must have been describing the Jerusalem visit Luke describes (without details that may be contradictory) in Acts 11:27–30. Whatever trip to Jerusalem may be referenced, this passage in Galatians reflects another position within the church about the church's relationship to and expectations of Gentile believers who did not conform to the law of circumcision, which some Christians believed to be mandatory behavior for those who believed in Jesus as the Christ.

Invite someone to read the following text aloud:

Galatians 2:1-10

¹Then after fourteen years I went up again to Jerusalem with Barnabas, taking Titus along with me. ²I went up in response to a revelation. Then I laid before them (though only in a private meeting with the acknowledged leaders) the gospel that I proclaim among the Gentiles, in order to make sure that I was not running, or had not run, in vain. ³But even Titus, who was with me, was not compelled to be circumcised, though he was a Greek. ⁴But because of false believers secretly brought in, who slipped in to spy on the freedom we have in Christ Jesus, so that they might enslave us— ⁵we did not submit to them even for a moment, so that the truth of the gospel might always remain with you. ⁶And from those who were supposed to be acknowledged leaders (what they actually were makes no difference to me; God shows no partiality)—those leaders contributed nothing to me. ⁷On the contrary, when they saw that I had been entrusted with the gospel for the uncircumcised, just as Peter had been entrusted with the gospel for the circumcised ⁸(for he who worked through Peter making him an apostle to the circumcised also worked through me in sending me to the Gentiles), ⁹and when James and Cephas and John, who were acknowledged pillars, recognized the grace that had been given to me, they gave to Barnabas and me the right hand of fellowship, agreeing that we should go to the Gentiles and they to the circumcised. ¹⁰They asked only one thing, that we remember the poor, which was actually what I was eager to do.

For discussion

(1) What does Paul mean by "the freedom we have in Christ" and "the truth of the gospel"? Why did Paul insist that submitting to be circumcised according to the law violated the work of Christ and the gospel with which he had been entrusted?

(2) How does Paul's account of his trip to meet with the Jerusalem leadership differ from Luke's account of the Jerusalem Council meeting in Acts 15? of Paul's visit to Jerusalem reported in Acts 11:27–30? Name various possible reasons for the differences in the reporting.

(3) Discuss to what extent you think the whole church needs to or is able to come to clear consensus about the gospel message to our church as we relate to lesbian and gay Christians? In light of Disciples' theology and polity, what principles of our life together should be reexamined and/or affirmed?

Personal Sharing

The question for consideration now is, What is the next step in our gospel journey as our church relates to gay and lesbian Christians? Regardless of where a congregation (group) is in its thinking after going through this process of discernment, an appropriate question related to our discernment question is, What is the gospel message to the church as we relate to lesbian and gay Christians?

Consider your response to the gospel message in the following ways:

Step 1: Building on what you shared in stage 5, brainstorm about the direction/actions to which your congregation (group) is being called by God. On a large newsprint flipchart or blackboard, list insights from members of the group that move the church toward further action in response to your hearing the gospel.

Step 2: Consider this list of questions that may help you consider the next part of your gospel journey.

a. Will we include or exclude lesbian and gay persons from baptism, the Lord's supper, or church membership?

b. What will we do with church members who come out as gay or lesbian? Will we affirm them as full members of the body of Christ, or will we practice some form of church discipline? What else would cause us to exercise church discipline, or will it be reserved only for gay and lesbian Christians?

c. What will be our expectations for the behavior of lesbian and gay Christians in the church? Counseling? Healing? Celibacy? Silence? Monogamy?

d. What forms of pastoral support will we offer to gay and lesbian Christians?

e. Will we enter into the process to become an open and affirming congregation? *(For resources contact your church's welcoming program, such as Open and Affirming Ministries. See list of Web sites at the end of this manual.)*

f. Will we support the ordination of lesbian and gay ministerial candidates?

g. Will we conscientiously disobey church policies if they disagree with our understanding?

h. Will we support or oppose civil rights for lesbians and for gay men?

i. How do we make our welcome or exclusion of gay and lesbian Christians clear in our worship, sermons, and prayers?

j. Can lesbian and gay Christians serve on committees and as elders, Sunday school teachers, deacons, and pastors?

k. Should gay and lesbian persons remain silent about their sexuality, or do we welcome them openly? Do we affirm their relationships? Do we celebrate holy unions?

l. How do we remain in Christian community with those with whom we disagree?

m. Do we need to address sexuality and sexual ethics for all people in our congregation, not just lesbian and gay Christians?

n. How will we advertise and make known our stance to include or exclude gay and lesbian Christians?

Step 3: Strategize as a group about ways you will effect the next gospel actions in your congregation. Determine accountability strategies to ensure follow-up to this discernment process.

Step 4: Examine the resource list at the end of this manual. Name other resources that might be helpful to your process. Contact your church's regional leaders for additional resources for the continuing journey.

CLOSING WORSHIP

HYMN

COMMUNION SERVICE

Words of Institution: 1 Corinthians 11:23–26
Prayer for the loaf and the cup
Partaking of the loaf and the cup

CLOSING PRAYER

BENEDICTION

As you depart, say to one another, "God be with you till we meet again."

Sending Forth and Consecration

OPENING WORSHIP

LITANY OF THE ONE SPIRIT

We call upon the Spirit of God to gather us together.
We honor the Spirit of God, dwelling in each of us.
We come to listen to one another.
And we come to listen for the Spirit who dwells within us all.
We honor this space as the place where God calls us together.
We cherish and protect what is shared in this space.
We find our unity in the One God, not in doctrine or argument.
We honor our unity in Christ.
To the One whom we honor and praise,
the One God who is Love. Amen.

INVOCATION (in unison)

O God, we have come together to walk with you, as did the disciples of old, along our own Emmaus Road. Our original fears and uncertainties have been replaced with the fresh wind of your Spirit. New challenges loom before us, put in place by the discerning of your Word. Bless the continuation of our journey, which in many ways has only just begun, in the simple and sacred act of the breaking of bread. Amen.

LIGHTING OF A CANDLE

> God's Word is a lamp to our feet
> **and a light to our path.**
> We light this candle to remind us that we do not make this journey alone.
> *[Light candle here.]*
> **May God light our way. Amen.**

STATEMENT OF COVENANT

God, as facilitator of this discussion, invites us to enter into a covenant with God and with one another.

In response to God's invitation:

I will honor and respect every participant as a person of faith.

I will claim a shared belief that the Holy Spirit is present and at work in this community.

I will examine the whole of scripture, not just isolated verses.

I will earnestly seek to hear and understand perspectives different from my own.

I will seek to retain a unity of Spirit even when I disagree.

As God's church, this will be a safe and confidential place where people can discuss sensitive issues freely without feeling that they will be attacked or rejected. Amen.

Bible Study: Romans 15:7–13

This section of Paul's letter to the Romans began in chapter 14:1–4.

> Welcome those who are weak in faith, but not for the purpose of quarreling over opinions. Some believe in eating anything, while the weak eat only vegetables. Those who eat must not despise those who abstain, and those who abstain must not pass judgment on those who eat; for God has welcomed them. Who are you to pass judgment on servants of another? It is before their own lord that they stand or fall. And they will be upheld, for the Lord is able to make them stand.

The Christian Church (Disciples of Christ) maintains as one of its main tenets the idea that each individual has the freedom and the responsibility of biblical interpretation and of a personal relationship with God through Jesus Christ, with which no one else has any right to dictate terms or to interfere. We are accorded liberty and competency in matters of faith. We will each "stand before our own Lord," and so we must accord a corresponding respect to all conscientious persons and positions even if, and especially when, they are not in accord with our own.

Invite someone to read the following text aloud:

Romans 15:7–13

Welcome one another, therefore, just as Christ has welcomed you, for the glory of God. For I tell you that Christ has become a servant of the circumcised on behalf of the truth of God in order that he might confirm the promises given to the patriarchs, and in order that the Gentiles might glorify God for God's mercy. As it is written, "Therefore I will confess you among the Gentiles, and sing praises to your name"; and again he says, "Rejoice, O Gentiles, with God's people"; and again, "Praise the Lord, all you Gentiles, and let all the peoples praise him"; and again Isaiah says, "The root of Jesse shall come, the one who rises to rule the Gentiles; in him the Gentiles shall hope." May the God of hope fill you with all joy and peace in believing, so that you may abound in hope by the power of the Holy Spirit.

For discussion

(1) In the context of Romans 14 and 15, what does Paul mean by the welcome of Christ and the admonition to welcome one another?

(2) Invite each person to share in this manner:

"I have been welcomed by Christ. I have experienced that welcome when…"

After each person shares, the group responds:

"[*Name*], May the God of hope fill you with all joy and peace in believing, so that you may abound in hope by the power of the Holy Spirit."

Personal Sharing

This stage is a time for reflection on the experience of the process as well as a time to celebrate its completion. A common meal or social time and worship experience will be helpful to give thanks for the discoveries made and bonds of friendship established.

Discuss the experience of the whole process. How has it affected you? What guidance have you received from the Holy Spirit? In what ways do you understand the question at a deeper level? Are there new questions that you want to explore? What do you think God wants for your church? How faithfully were you able to keep the covenant and the rules for discernment? What other issues in the church will you be able to explore in this manner?

CLOSING WORSHIP

HYMN

COMMUNION SERVICE

The discernment process is not complete until we give thanks for Christ's presence and grace and for the work of the Holy Spirit among us. The act of coming together at the Lord's table reminds us that as people of the table we are bound together even in the midst of our differences.

Words of Institution: 1 Corinthians 11:23–26
Prayer for the loaf and the cup
Partaking of the loaf and the cup.

A PRAYER OF THANKSGIVING

Form a circle and give members the opportunity to offer their thanks on these topics and others they may wish to share.

- For completing the process

- For new insights received

- For staying together through the process

- For the presence and gifts of the Holy Spirit

BENEDICTION

Each person is invited to take a piece of the jigsaw puzzle as he or she departs. Say to one another, "As members of the body of Christ, bound together by the Spirit of God, I pray that God will be with you until we meet again."

Hymn Suggestions

Ruth Fletcher, in *Take, Break, Receive,* suggests hymns from *Chalice Hymnal* that are good for use in a discernment process. You may want to use these in your closing worship times at the end of each session.

236	Wind Who Makes All Winds That Blow
241	Holy Spirit, Truth Divine
242	Shaping Spirit, Move Among Us
244	Loving Spirit
254	Breathe on Me, Breath of God
258	Holy Wisdom
259	Spirit of the Living God
265	Spirit of God, Descend upon My Heart
266	Gracious Spirit, Dwell with Me
269	Come, Holy Spirit, Fill This Place
288	O God of Vision
321	Break Thou the Bread of Life
348	More About Jesus Would I Know
354	Seek Ye First
461	Lord, Whose Love Through Humble Service
463	Renew Your Church
464	God of Grace and God of Glory
465	We Are Called to Follow Jesus

Bibliography

This is not meant to be an exhaustive bibliography, as there are many, many books on the issues surrounding gay men and women and the church, including books about the Bible, theology, sexuality, ethics, and more. The following list is intended to be a broad sampling of books that are relevant to the question, What is the gospel message to our church as we relate to gay and lesbian Christians? as well as resources for facilitating exploration of that question. All who have an opinion on this subject will find resources here that they agree with and resources that they disagree with. It is our hope that you will find something here to further your understanding of church and gospel.

Bible Study Resources

Helminiak, Daniel A. *What the Bible Really Says about Homosexuality.* San Francisco: Alamo Square Press, 2000. An in-depth study of Romans, placing the scripture deep within its cultural and biblical contexts, shows how we often misread Paul.

Osterman, Mary Jo. *Claiming the Promise: An Ecumenical Welcoming Bible Study Resource on Homosexuality.* Chicago: Reconciling Congregations Program, 1997. A study program created by programs from several denominations working for the affirmation of gay men and women in the church. Useful for a church Sunday school or Bible study group. Purchase information can be found at http://gladalliance.org/claimingthepromise.html

Soards, Marion L. *Scripture and Homosexuality: Biblical Authority and the Church Today.* Louisville: Westminster John Knox Press, 1995. Written from a Presbyterian perspective, this book discusses many of the familiar texts considered relevant to the debate concerning homosexuality and the church.

Homosexuality and the Church

Grenz, Stanley J. *Welcoming But Not Affirming: An Evangelical Response to Homosexuality.* Louisville: Westminster John Knox Press, 1998. Written from the evangelical viewpoint, discusses how the church can welcome gay persons without affirming gay unions and homosexual behavior.

Hefling, Charles, ed. *Our Selves, Our Souls and Bodies.* Boston: Cowley Publications, 1996. A collection of essays and reflections from many perspectives, including family, scripture, and theology, but always with a personal, thoughtful touch. Written from the Episcopalian perspective, but solid reading for all Christians.

Holben, L. R. *What Christians Think About Homosexuality.* N. Richland Hills, Tex.: D & F Scott, 1999. Presents six different Christian viewpoints concerning homosexuality and the church, including the arguments for and against each opinion.

Schmidt, Thomas E. *Straight and Narrow? Compassion and Clarity in the Homosexuality Debate.* Downers Grove, Ill.: InterVarsity Press, 1995. From an evangelical viewpoint, surveys biblical studies and science to argue that homosexuality is both sinful and harmful.

Seow, Choon-Leong, ed. *Homosexuality and Christian Community.* Louisville: Westminster John Knox Press, 1996. Written by faculty from the Princeton Theological Seminary, an academic but readable set of essays on scripture, theology, and faithful Christian practice from a variety of perspectives. Includes an excellent chapter entitled "How to Discuss Moral Issues Surrounding Homosexuality When You Know You Are Right."

Homosexuality and Faith

Wink, Walter, ed. *Homosexuality and Christian Faith.* Minneapolis: Fortress Press, 1999. A collection of reflections on the Bible, faith, and personal experience. Presents a range of viewpoints from a wide range of perspectives.

The Church's Response to Gay Men and Women

Dallas, Joe. *A Strong Delusion: Confronting the "Gay Christian" Movement.* Eugene, Oreg.: Harvest House Publishers, 1996. Argues against the acceptance of homosexuality in the church, using biblical responses to pro-gay arguments and providing advice to bring this message to gay people.

Scanzoni, Letha Dawson, and Virginia Ramey Mollenkott. *Is the Homosexual My Neighbor?: A Positive Christian Response.* San Francisco: Harper, 1994. A classic on spirituality and the affirmative Christian response to gay men and women, this book covers not only biblical and theological issues but also topics such as gays in the military, the AIDS crisis, and genetic research on homosexuality.

Waun, Maurine. *More than Welcome: Learning to Embrace Gay, Lesbian, Bisexual, and Transgendered Persons in the Church.* St. Louis: Chalice Press, 1999. A pastor draws on her own experiences in sharing the compelling stories of specific men and women of her acquaintance who, only because they happened to be gay, have been marginalized or even condemned by the churches into which they should have been welcomed.

Change Ministries

Paulk, John, and Anne Paulk. *Love Won Out.* Colorado Springs: Focus on the Family Publishing, 1999. The story of two people who left homosexuality, found each other, and married, presented as an argument that gay men and women can and should change.

White, Mel. *Stranger at the Gate: To Be Gay and Christian in America.* New York: Plume, 1995. The author, formerly a ghostwriter for Jerry Falwell, Pat Robertson, and Billy Graham, writes of his attempt to live as a straight person, including twenty-five years of marriage and two children, and his conclusion along with his wife that they needed to end their marriage and that he needed to come out of the closet.

(See also "Answers to Your Questions about Sexual Orientation and Homosexuality," listed below.)

Sexuality and Spirituality

Mollenkott, Virginia Ramey. *Omnigender: A Trans-Religious Approach.* Cleveland: Pilgrim Press, 2001. The author writes that our common understanding of gender is woefully inadequate. She honors the experiences of people who do not fit within the traditional binary concept of gender, shows that

this concept of gender is oppressive, and offers a new, more
flexible gender paradigm.

Nelson, James B. *The Intimate Connection: Male Sexuality, Masculine
Spirituality.* Philadelphia: Westminster Press, 1988. Using
insights he gained from the feminist revolution, the author
explores issues of intimacy and sexuality for men, seeking an
understanding of the meaning of love.

Smedes, Lewis B. *Sex for Christians.* Grand Rapids, Mich.:
Eerdmans, 1971. Discusses sex and sexuality from an
evangelical perspective.

Homosexuality and Science

"Answers to Your Questions about Sexual Orientation and
Homosexuality." American Psychological Association, 2001. A
scientific perspective from the American Psychological
Association on homosexuality and sexuality. On the Web at
http://www.apa.org/pubinfo/orient.html.

Jones, Stanton L., and Mark A. Yarhouse. *Homosexuality: The Use of
Scientific Research in the Church's Moral Debate.* Downers Grove,
Ill.: InterVarsity Press, 2000. Reviews scientific research on
homosexuality through a conservative lens, which begins with
the premise that homosexuality is immoral.

Discussing Homosexuality

"Talking Together as Christians about Homosexuality: A Guide for
Congregations." Evangelical Lutheran Church in America,
1999. A discussion guide for congregations, along with a
leader's guide, that fosters conversations about homosexuality.
The leader's guide includes a useful page on "Guidelines for
Talking about Homosexuality." This resource can be
downloaded for free from
http://www.elca.org/dcs/talking.html

Gaede, Beth Ann, ed. *Congregations Talking about Homosexuality.*
Bethesda, Md.: Alban Institute, 1998. From the Alban
Institute, a resource for those working to start a dialog within
their congregations. Includes stories of congregational
experiences, tips for getting started, and guidelines to keep the
dialog constructive.

(See also Choon-Leong Seow's *Homosexuality and Christian
Community* listed above.)

Discernment

Fletcher, Ruth. *Take, Break, Receive: The Practice of Discernment in the Christian Church (Disciples of Christ)*. Indianapolis: Division of Homeland Ministries, 1999. A resource on the spiritual practice of discernment in the Christian tradition applied to the congregational life of the Christian Church. Includes a useful chapter on "The Leader's Toolbox" as well as resources for discernment in *Chalice Hymnal*. Available from Homeland Ministries.

Johnson, Luke Timothy. *Scripture and Discernment: Decision Making in the Church*. Nashville: Abingdon Press, 1996. Starting with the authority of scripture, describes discernment as a response to God's activity in the world that moves us to decision.

Diversity

Law, Eric H. F. *Inclusion: Making Room for Grace*. St. Louis: Chalice Press, 2000. A concise, biblically based, readable discussion of the social and theological issues concerning inclusion and exclusion of all kinds in the church. Includes discussions of the tension between law and grace and excellent suggestions for improving a congregation's ability to include others without losing its own integrity.

Web Resources

If you are having difficulty finding gay voices to participate in your process, below is a list of gay Christian Web sites that might be able to help you. As has already been mentioned, it is important for the gay voices to be heard for the discernment process to have integrity.

Open & Affirming (Christian Church Disciples of Christ)
http://gladalliance.org/oaa.html

Open and Affirming (United Church of Christ)
http://www.ucccoalition.org/programs/onahtmlpages.htm

Reconciling in Christ Program (Lutheran)
http://www.lcna.org/riclist.html

More Light Presbyterians (PCUSA) *http://www.mlp.org/find.html*

Welcoming and Affirming Baptists (American Baptist Convention)
http://members.aol.com/wabaptists/memlist.html

Affirming Congregations (United Church of Canada)
http://www.affirmunited.org/UCaclist.htm

Brethren/Mennonite Council for Lesbian and Gay Concerns
http://webcom.com/bmc/scn.html

Integrity (Episcopal) *http://integrityusa.org/chapters/index.htm*

Dignity (Roman Catholic) *http://www.dignityusa.org/chapters.html*